# smart
# closet
# makeovers

by Cynthia Overbeck Bix ▪ Sunset Books, Menlo Park, California

# contents

## SUNSET BOOKS

V.P., GENERAL MANAGER
Richard A. Smeby

V.P., EDITORIAL DIRECTOR
Bob Doyle

PRODUCTION DIRECTOR
Lory Day

OPERATIONS DIRECTOR
Rosann Sutherland

MARKETING MANAGER
Linda Barker

ART DIRECTOR
Vasken Guiragossian

SPECIAL SALES
Brad Moses

### Staff for this book

MANAGING EDITOR
Jennifer Block Martin

SENIOR EDITOR
Ben Marks

COPY EDITOR/INDEXER
Phyllis Elving

ART DIRECTOR
Vasken Guiragossian

PRINCIPAL PHOTOGRAPHER
Michele Lee Willson

PHOTOGRAPHY STYLISTS
Laura Del Fava, Julie Maldonado

PRINCIPAL ILLUSTRATOR
Tracy La Rue Hohn

PAGE PRODUCTION
Linda Bouchard, Susan Paris

ASSOCIATE EDITOR
Carrie Dodson Davis

PREPRESS COORDINATOR
Danielle Johnson

PROOFREADER
Michelle Pollace

CLOSET CONSULTANT
ShipShape

Cover photograph courtesy of
Schulte Distinctive Storage.

10 9 8 7 6 5 4 3 2
First printing June 2006
Copyright © 2006 Sunset Publishing
Corporation, Menlo Park, CA 94025.
All rights reserved, including the right of
reproduction in whole or in part in any form.

ISBN-13: 978-0-376-01114-5
ISBN-10: 0-376-01114-9
Library of Congress Control Number:
2006922885
Printed in the United States.

For additional copies of *Smart Closet
Makeovers* or any other Sunset book,
visit us at www.sunsetbooks.com or
call 1-800-526-5111.

# introduction

WHETHER YOU LIVE IN A SPACIOUS HOUSE or a studio apartment, a cozy cottage or an airy loft, you probably wish you had more—or at least better—closet space. Well, wish no more. Using simple methods and readily available components, you can create the handsome, functional closets that you really want. Read on to learn how your bedroom closet can be transformed from drab to absolutely fab; how a rarely used storage closet can be turned into an efficient home office; how space-hogging washers and dryers can be tucked away behind closet doors. You'll find inspiring before-and-after photos, easy-to-follow step-by-step building instructions, and a bonus chapter devoted to terrific organizing ideas for the entire home.

## THE SMART CLOSET

From the spacious walk-in clothes closet to the narrow utility closet, a smart closet is all of these things:

**ORDERLY** Give your madness a method: Categorize everything. In a utility closet, group cleaning products together on a shelf, electrical cords in a container. Arrange the linen closet so sheets are stacked in sets, towels according to color. If you create space for each category of items, you stand a better chance of finding what you're looking for when you really need it.

**ACCESSIBLE** Arrange the contents so everything is easy to locate. What's not in plain sight should be neatly stashed in clearly labeled containers. Position everyday items in front; stow things that are used less frequently farther back.

**EASY TO MAINTAIN** Choose an organization system that suits your personality and your habits. An intrinsically neat person will lovingly store each pair of shoes in its own labeled box, while a chronically rushed person would probably rather set shoes on accessible shelves so they can grab and go.

**FLEXIBLE** Devise an adaptable system that will keep pace with your lifestyle changes. A flexibly designed closet can roll with the punches, accommodating new items and purposes.

**CREATIVE** Be resourceful. Use umbrella stands to hold wrapping paper, baskets for rolled towels, pant hangers for linens. Don't forget the closet's walls and door—perfect places for hooks, racks, and other storage accessories.

**EFFICIENT** Make every nook and cranny work for you. If a shelf is so high up that your stuff is inaccessible, either lower it or attach a hanging basket and fill it with frequently used items. If one rod isn't enough, position a second below it for pants folded over wood hangers.

getting started

## 1 FIRST

# set your objectives

YOU'VE DECIDED TO REORGANIZE YOUR CLOSET—CONGRATULATIONS! But before you start dragging out every last item, take a step back and decide precisely what purpose you want your closet to serve. Your answer might be as simple as a place to store clothes or a spot in which to corral the kids' toys. Or, you might have something more elaborate in mind, like a built-in office. Next, envision what the closet will hold. Don't be afraid to dream big—you may find that a newly organized closet has more room than you would have thought. Whatever your end goal might be, you're not alone.

**MAKEOVER CANDIDATES**
*The closet opposite is ready for its makeover, but the closet above probably looks more familiar. It's stuffed to the gills, which is a problem that won't be solved by space-saving components alone. It's time to face your demons and get to work!*

Everyone has at least one closet that could use a little attention. It's how you tackle the skeletons in your closet that makes the difference. The next few pages will guide you through the process of creating a smart closet of your own, using a real-life makeover as an example.

# SECOND

# take inventory, then purge

I t's a simple choice: stuff or space. The more things you possess, the less space you have at your disposal and the less flexibility you have when you want to add or rearrange things. Take a good hard look at all of your possessions to determine if they are worth the space they consume.

**PLAN AHEAD** Set aside a realistic block of time so that you can really get down to business without being interrupted. Designate a staging area where you can sort stuff into piles as you work. If you're tackling a clothes closet, you'll need a place to hang clothes, such as a portable rack or spare bed, where you can lay them out.

**EMPTY IT** That's right, remove everything, including the hangers, your old scrapbook, that pile of blankets, all of your shoes, the works. Move everything to the staging area.

**CATEGORIZE** An essential principle of organizing is the concept of categories. Everything you own can be assigned a category—linens,

## quick tip

Another approach is to empty out all your closets in order to get a complete overview of your stuff. You'll undoubtedly find items from a single category scattered in several places. Eliminate duplicates and choose a closet for what's left.

craft materials, and sports gear. Divide broad categories like clothing into subcategories (shoes, out-of-season clothes, hats). You

may also want to bundle things like package-wrapping supplies (paper, tape, scissors, ribbon) or electrical items (cords, lightbulbs, plugs, batteries) into categories of their own.

**REMOVE STOWAWAYS** Just because something is in a particular closet doesn't mean it should remain there—a winter blanket that you stuffed in your bedroom closet

**GET ORGANIZED**
*In the staging area, the* Smart Closet Makeovers *team sorted this closet's items into categories—office, craft/hobby, cleaning, clothing, documents.*

when the weather turned warm belongs in the linen closet. Return stowaway items to their rightful homes, then survey the rest of your house for items that might logically belong in this closet.

**PARE DOWN** If you're waffling on a piece of clothing, ask yourself these questions: Have I worn it in the last year? Does it look good? Does it fit? Is it in good condition? For other items, ask: Do I use it regularly (or in season)? Is it beautiful or pleasurable to look at? Does it have meaning for me? If your answer to most of these questions is yes, then keep it. If not, box it, bag it, and haul it to the curb. That's right, out it goes. Banish second thoughts.

**CLEAN** Wipe down the closet's walls and mop or vacuum the floor. Wearing gloves, remove any mildew from the walls by sponging on a mixture of ½ cup chlorine bleach, ⅓ cup powdered laundry detergent, and 1 gallon hot water. Wipe off with a clean, damp sponge. If you are planning to paint, choose an interior mold- and mildew-resistant type.

**STRATEGIZE** Now decide where you will store each category of items. Many closets can easily do double or even triple duty—the high shelves in a kid's closet may be perfect for storing holiday decorations, for instance.

## out it goes

Parting is such sweet sorrow—but it can also put a little cash in your pocket. Here are some options:

**Sell it at a store.** Local stores specializing in used books, CDs, sports equipment, and so forth may buy items from you outright. Consignment shops can be a good option for gently worn designer clothing two seasons to two years old. The shop usually sets the price. You can expect to receive between 40 and 50 percent of the proceeds for those items that sell.

**Sell it on the Internet.** Opt for a classifieds site in your region if you want the buyer to pick up the items in person. Or go for the highest bidder in an online auction. These sites usually give clear parameters as to what goods qualify and how they should be priced; you will be responsible for shipping and possibly sales tax. If the process seems daunting, look for a service that manages the sale for you in exchange for a percentage of the proceeds.

**Hold a tag sale.** This takes lots of work but can be a fun event. You'll need to advertise your sale, sort and price your wares, have cash on hand for change, and be prepared to bargain.

**Donate it.** Giving things away may be the simplest way to go—and you can take a tax deduction for contributions to nonprofit organizations. For example, your extra towels and blankets can mean a lot to the local shelter.

**Toss or recycle.** Some things are just too old or worn even to be given away. Throw them in the trash or recycling bin—they had a good life.

# THIRD

# measure everything

Once you've emptied your closet and thinned out your belongings, it's time to find out how much space you have to work with. Make a front-view sketch of the closet, including the doorframe (see the drawing below). Take careful measurements to the nearest $\frac{1}{16}$ inch and record them on your sketch. Note any obstacles that may affect your closet layout, such as exposed ductwork, a slanted ceiling, or electrical outlets.

### COMMON CLOSETS

To determine how many feet of rod and shelving you'll need, take stock of what you want to store. For a clothes closet, which should be at least 24 inches deep (28 inches for bulky coats), the amount of rod you'll need is determined by more than just the closet's width. Shirts, skirts, and slacks can hang in multiple rows, one above the other, which adds to your overall rod length. Also assess how much space you need for folded clothing, shoes, accessories (neckties, handbags, belts), and large items such as tote bags or hats. Garments you wear frequently should be within easy reach (the average maximum reach is 77 inches high for women, 83 inches for men).

For a linen closet, stack and measure folded towels, bedding, pillows, and whatever else you plan to store in there.

If you're making over a utility closet, calculate the space required for your vacuum cleaner, broom, mop, and cleaning supplies.

For offices in closets, measure both the depth and width of file cabinets. To make sure drawers won't be impeded by the closet doorframe, measure cabinet depth with a drawer fully extended.

▶ **INSIDE DIMENSIONS**
*When measuring your closet, don't forget both sides of the inside doorframe, which can get in the way of components with drawers, or the baseboards, which can reduce a closet's floor dimensions by a critical half inch or more.*

Width
Height
Height
Depth
Width
Door to wall

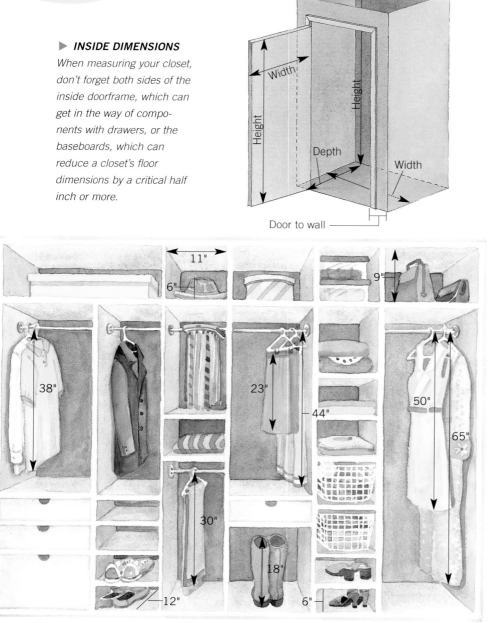

◀ **MEASURE GARMENTS**
*When planning your closet, take into account the standard space requirements for storing various types of clothing and accessories.*

▶ **ADULTS**

*Put the things you use often between waist and eye level. Position shelves so all family members can reach what they need.*

▼ **KIDS**

*A good rule of thumb is to put toys on the bottom shelf near the floor where most kids play.*

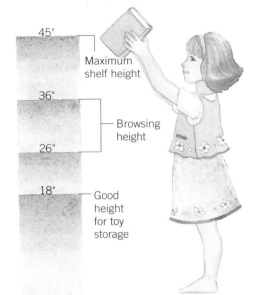

45"
Maximum shelf height

36"
Browsing height

26"

18"
Good height for toy storage

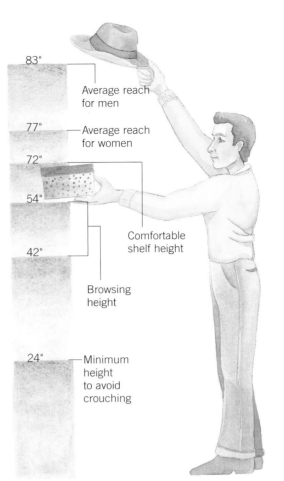

83"
Average reach for men

77"
Average reach for women

72"

54"
Comfortable shelf height

42"
Browsing height

24"
Minimum height to avoid crouching

## skills and tools

Most closet makeovers are not that complicated. In many cases you can achieve major improvements by purchasing a few containers and a couple of products designed to help your closet work smarter. Even if your closet requires more attention—such as installing new rods or shelves—you'd be surprised how easy it is to design and execute the makeover yourself.

Begin by taking stock of your building skills and available tools. If you are comfortable taking measurements, reading a level, and using a drill and a hammer, you'll be able to tackle almost any closet project. You can do a lot with a cordless drill and an assortment of bits; an electronic stud finder (models that also locate electrical conduits are best); two screwdrivers (one standard, one Phillips); and a selection of nails, screws, and fasteners such as toggle and anchor bolts. Most shelves are sold in precut widths, eliminating the need to make difficult lengthwise cuts, and many lumber yards will even make your crosscuts for you for a nominal fee.

To learn more about basic closet carpentry, turn to pages 80–87.

CORDLESS DRILL

CARPENTER'S LEVEL

TAPE MEASURE

# shop for a system

Having assessed your skills and made your measurements, you're ready to improve upon the old single-rod-and-shelf configuration common to so many homes. Fortunately the wealth of prefab systems, freestanding units, and movable components—from file cabinets to baskets—will enable you to devise a design that's right for you and your closet.

**WHERE AND WHAT TO BUY**

Hardware stores, online retailers, home-improvement centers, and specialty stores that feature closet systems offer coated-wire or melamine shelf-and-bracket systems. These systems range from modest to high-end in both style and cost.

Before you purchase anything, have your rough closet sketch in hand, complete with measurements. Identify your goals, too (storage for winter coats, a mini-office). Take advantage of in-store consultants who can help you plan a layout and determine which components you'll need. Components generally come with assembly instructions, but not necessarily all the required tools and hardware. Some stores offer installation for an additional fee, while others are happy to teach you the basics of installing their systems so that you can do it yourself.

▼ *COATED WIRE*
*Wire systems are easy to install and kindest to tight budgets.*

# ...or mix 'n' match

If you're not handy with tools or if you're a renter, you may find that a few strategically placed products can bring order to chaos.

Boxes, bins, buckets, shoe racks, file boxes, magazine butlers—these hardworking storage components can be found in a wealth of materials, sizes, colors, and configurations. Use them in creative ways—a plastic sweater box can work equally well for stationery supplies, while a shoe cubby may be perfect for toys.

If you want more shelving but don't want to build it in, consider tucking in a freestanding bookcase. A stand-alone piece like a chest of drawers can work just as well inside a closet as out.

Canvas pockets, cubbies, and bags that hang from closet rods present a neat storage solution for everything from sweaters to papers. For more ideas, turn to page 96.

**▲ MELAMINE**
*This solid material presents a clean, simple look and offers such hardware options as the retractable shelf shown here.*

**WIRE** Vinyl- or epoxy-coated steel is usually the most economical choice and offers great versatility. The open grids allow air circulation and visibility of contents. If you will be storing small, loose objects or worry that grids may leave indentations in fabrics, buy shelf liners. Wire systems are long-lasting, won't warp, and can handle a fair amount of weight. Several manufacturers are going beyond basic white and offering colored coating and nickel finishes.

**MELAMINE** Offered by most closet companies, ready-to-assemble (RTA) melamine systems are constructed of particle board coated with an outer layer of resin. The best melamine is a thermally fused ¾-inch board. Lesser-quality melamine, found in some home centers, is usually ⅝-inch board that has been cold-pressed. Both types come in white, off-white, or wood-grain.

To learn how to assemble standard melamine components, turn to page 86.

**INSTALLATION OPTIONS** Some systems hang from wall-mounted tracks. These hanging systems are versatile and can support plenty of weight. Be sure to ask if your system must be attached to wall studs or if it can be anchored to drywall or masonry. To learn how to install a wall-mounted system, turn to page 84.

Freestanding components require level floors, so they're not always good for carpeted rooms. In these situations, consider a system that is braced between the ceiling and the floor. For freestanding options, turn to page 98.

# FIFTH

# put it all together

Now that you've learned how to take inventory, purge, measure, and shop, you're ready for your makeover. The guest-room closet shown here is a good example. It needed to house a variety of items: clothing, vacuum, ironing board, past years' tax records, office supplies, photos, and more. The challenge was fitting everything back in without sacrificing accessibility. Apply these lessons to create your own smart closet, anywhere in your home.

**BEFORE**

It may not look like much, but the fact that the closet above was filled with items stored in boxes and bins—most of which dated from a not-so-recent move—was a step in the right direction. The closet's rudimentary organization made it relatively easy for the *Smart Closet Makeovers* team to clean things out. The team moved everything to a staging area (see photo on page 8) for sorting or removal.

**A FRESH START**

After a coat of mildew-resistant wall paint, white wire shelving was installed (left). This system was chosen for its flexibility and low cost. Along with flat wire shelves, some basket shelves on the right side of the closet were installed to contain small items. On the left, space was set aside for two levels of closet rods.

**LET IT EVOLVE**

The new closet's design improved through experimentation. The initial plan (left) was to hang special-occasion clothes from two rods on the left side. After consideration, the team decided that those clothes would be moved to another closet to make way for craft materials, gift wrap, and office supplies. One rod remains for guests.

## AFTER: ADMIRE YOUR MAKEOVER

In the newly organized closet, every item is categorized in a labeled container, and every category has a permanent home. Craft supplies, stashed in plastic bins, occupy the closet's lower left side. Above them is a hanging gift-wrap organizer. On the right are office supplies in assorted open containers, as well as covered bins and boxes. Albums and photo boxes are clustered on the shelf above.

In the middle, an eight-drawer wire tower houses linens; casters allow for easy repositioning. A vacuum cleaner and an ironing board occupy an easy-access open space. The sturdy top shelf holds rarely used items—camping gear and tax returns.

Everything is clearly labeled, making it a snap to return items to their rightful homes, thus preserving the closet's organizational integrity. Many of the new boxes are either transparent, allowing quick identification of the contents within, or came with built-in label holders (the team used a handheld electronic labeler to identify "sheets," "this year's taxes," and so on). As for the closet's doors, they were removed entirely so that the closet's contents were always handy.

smart
closets

NOW THAT YOU'RE READY to make over your own closet, it's time for a little inspiration, as well as some practical ideas for specific situations. On the following pages, you'll discover smart solutions for organizing just about every closet type and configuration. You'll find examples of efficient closets in high-traffic areas of the home, from the foyer to kids' rooms to the kitchen. You'll also see closets dedicated to more specialized needs, including offices, craft centers, and laundry areas. The *Smart Closet Makeovers* team tackled a variety of closets in need of change. While some blossomed with the addition of just a few key products and components designed to maintain order, others required a complete overhaul and a change of scope. Yours may fall somewhere in between. If so, check out the Closet Sketchbook design alternatives that accompany many of the team's makeovers, because one size does not fit all.

**MAKEOVER MARVELS**

*The revamped closet on the facing page dedicates one shelf for guests, while the rest of its space is in constant use as an office supply area—you can have it both ways when your closet is organized. Above, curtains replaced sliding mirrored doors as part of a bedroom closet makeover.*

# inviting entryway

Where do you stow all the gear—boots, backpacks, umbrellas, jackets, strollers—that travels in and out of the house with you every day? It all goes in the entry closet, of course. As shown by the closet on these two pages, you can install hooks, racks, pegs, or clips to hang everything from dog leashes to keys. Tame tangles of scarves, mittens, and sports equipment by providing an assortment of bins and baskets for you and your guests. Add extra shelves or move high ones down so children and short adults can reach them. Use a shoe rack with catch tray below to ensure that mud doesn't get tracked through the house. And be sure to leave a few sturdy hangers free for your guests' coats.

## THE MAKEOVER

### OBJECTIVES
- Maximize space
- Assign areas for coats, shoes, keys, and dog gear

### IMPROVEMENTS
- Built new shelf
- Culled jackets to make room for guest coats
- Affixed key racks
- Organized pet supplies
- Added umbrella stand and rack for wet shoes

**BEFORE** The typical entry-hall closet below featured a single rod topped by a lone shelf—and lots of wasted space above and below. A recessed area hidden from view to the right was largely inaccessible, even though it held oft-used phone books. Shoes and various odds and ends were jumbled on the floor. The dog's scattered paraphernalia prompted a frantic search before every walk.

**HARDWORKING CORNER** There's a whole lot going on in one corner of this closet. Winter coats hang from matching wooden hangers; all the ingredients for the daily dog walk—tennis balls, plastic bags, treats—are close at hand; and keys are neatly organized and labeled on hooks just inside the door.

**AFTER** The *Smart Closet Makeovers* team asked the owners of this entry closet to take a hard look at their accumulated collection of outerwear, resulting in a trip to Goodwill. This created room for guest coats. Shoes and boots stay tidy on a wooden rack; the lacquer tray catches drips on rainy days. Umbrellas are stowed in a cheery enameled metal holder. The team installed a new wood shelf for bike helmets, gloves, and scarves above the existing one. In the doggy department, dispersed items were brought to heel: leashes on easy-to-reach hooks on the back of the door, towels on the lower shelf for cleanup after muddy walks.

### CLOSET SKETCHBOOK

There's more than one way to organize an entry closet that has to store a lot in a small space. In this alternative plan, shelves tucked against the left wall hold bins for scarves, gloves, and other cold-weather gear. Hooks on the inside of the door supplement rod space. A freestanding drawer unit offers additional storage.

# divide and conquer

If your entry closet is home to everything from the vacuum cleaner to that 12-pack of paper towels, think geometrically. Dividing it both vertically and horizontally creates an attractive and orderly space—an organizing technique that works equally well for open or freestanding storage areas.

**EASY ACCESS** Open storage, either built-in or created with ready-to-assemble (RTA) components from a home center, is a good alternative when you don't have a traditional entry closet. It's also ideal for a mudroom off the back door or garage. The shallow doorless closets shown here make good use of hooks and cubbies to organize outerwear, shoes, and sports equipment. The closet at left features corkboard on one end so family members can post reminders of events or leave messages for each other. The baskets on top are for infrequently used items. In the closet above, baskets placed lower put scarves and gloves within easy reach.

**MULTIPURPOSE STORAGE** The small closet on this page has the big job of storing everything from coats to cleaning supplies. Dividing the space was the key to fitting it all in. Now coats go on one side, and a vacuum and ironing board occupy the other. A specialized holder keeps the iron handy and its cord tidy. Matching baskets group cleaning products, scarves, and other small items, giving the closet's varied contents an organized look. The topmost shelf is dedicated to overnight bags and totes, while a caddy hanging on the inside of the closet door holds gloves, an umbrella, and a yoga mat in a mesh bag.

# say curtains to mirrored doors

Even a modest bedroom closet is a pleasure to use when clothing and accessories are ready to wear and easy to find. Give hanging clothes room to breathe, and they will be simple to sort through and remain wrinkle free. Pile folded garments neatly (but not too high) on shelves using dividers to prevent stacks from collapsing on one another. Place handbags and other frequently used accessories where you can grab them and go. Divide your space with a combination of vertical partitions, shelves, drawers, and racks to help you get the most out of every square inch.

## THE MAKEOVER

**OBJECTIVE**

- **Create an easily accessible closet with a softer look**

**IMPROVEMENTS**

- **Removed mirrored doors**
- **Installed wrought-iron rod, hung drapes**
- **Reorganized clothing, shoes, and accessories**
- **Rearranged room to create a sitting area**

**BEFORE** This wide closet stretches across an entire bedroom wall, but its sliding mirrored doors—though they did make the small space feel bigger—overwhelmed the room and permitted access to only one side of the closet at a time.

**AFTER** To add style, texture, and color to her bedroom, the homeowner took the bold step of replacing her closet's mirrored doors with curtains—filmy sheers framed by rich red cotton, all hung from a single hand-wrought rod. When the curtains are closed, this part of the room is transformed into a comfortable sitting area.

**STYLISH SHOWCASE** After the homeowner reconfigured the rods and melamine shelves to better suit her wardrobe, the *Smart Closet Makeovers* team rearranged clothing and put accessories on display. Handbags and hats now get their own shelves, as do boots and shoes, with room set aside for new acquisitions. Wicker baskets, neatly labeled, hold scarves and belts. Jewelry is safe in a decorative dresser-top cabinet when it's not dangling from the arms of an artist's mannequin.

# neat and simple

A well-organized reach-in closet offers everything at a glance. If yours has sliding doors (which typically obscure half the closet from view), consider trading them for hinged or bifold doors. For the space-starved, hinged doors have the added merit of providing another surface on which to hang racks or mount hooks.

**BEFORE AND AFTER** Sliding doors on the small closet below made access to contents difficult (the open door seen on the right leads to another room). Overnight bags threatened to slide off the closet's narrow top shelf, and the entire lower half of the closet had become a dumping ground. New bifold doors open to reveal an organized, highly functional space. Using an RTA melamine system, the owners divided the closet vertically with a tower of cubbies. In lieu of drawers, baskets store shirts, folded sweaters, and other garments. On the right, tiered rods afford twice the hanging space for shirts and pants; the single rod at left accommodates long dresses and blouses. Infrequently used items go up on top.

## THE MAKEOVER

OBJECTIVE

- Reorganize space so all contents are efficiently stored and accessible

IMPROVEMENTS

- Replaced sliding doors with twin bifolds
- Installed melamine shelf system
- Replaced single long rod with three shorter ones

# handling handbags

Large or small, handbags can present a real storage challenge. Their varying shapes and sizes require creative solutions to keep them in order. The easiest way to store handbags in a closet is to line them up on a shelf, preferably at eye level and separated by shelf dividers. But if shelf space is limited, there are clever alternatives.

Hang bags from S-hooks (available at hardware stores), or save rod space by hanging a chain and hooking S-hooks through its links to create a vertical display. Towel racks attached to the wall or the back of the door can also accommodate S-hooks. And many over-the-door racks with built-in hooks work fine for handbags. You can also hang bags

from a ceiling-mounted pot rack or from hooks attached up the edge of a shelving tower or the inside of your closet's doorframe.

If a handbag coordinates with a specific outfit, hang it right on the same hanger with the garment. That way, you're ready to go at a moment's notice, accessories and all.

Some closet systems feature open wall-hung bins in which you can stash handbags. If you're concerned about dust, use see-through plastic boxes or labeled covered baskets. To keep empty handbags from losing their shape, stuff them with crumpled tissue paper.

# within reach

When all is said and done, a closet is little more than rect-angular recess in a wall. Despite this simplicity, there are nearly endless possibilities for configuring a closet's interior space, using either manufactured closet systems or custom construction. Shown here are two excellent configurations for a typical reach-in clothes closet. This type usually has doors, but it can also be open like the one on the facing page.

**CLEVER CORNER** Taking advantage of this closet's generous depth, an L-shaped storage area was created. The melamine system tucks in a double row of rods on the left, along with another facing front. Padded hangers protect delicate clothing from snagging, and keep silky tops from slipping off. Arranging shoes at eye-level saves time when assembling outfits.

**GARMENT GRID** The custom-built closet at right combines great design with loads of storage. Six equal sections, each equipped with a rod, allow systematic division of clothing according to color and garment type (white blouses in one section, jackets in another). The narrowly spaced shelves eliminate the problem of teetering stacks of clothing.

## stowing stuff

Belts and scarves, jewelry, lingerie and hosiery—although they are integral parts of a wardrobe, all too often they wind up in tangles or, worse, disappear. Throw out or donate what you don't use and store the rest so that it's readily accessible. You'll find specialty hangers for belts and scarves, and hanging bags with see-through pockets for jewelry, hosiery, and hair accessories. (If you prefer to keep your jewelry hidden, look for drawer inserts, or roll jewels in padded silverware bags and tuck them into a drawer.) Assorted hooks and racks—try a towel rack—are quick to install on the wall or door. Pegboard with removable hooks and trays is another option. For handbag storage, turn to page 25; for men's accessories, turn to page 34.

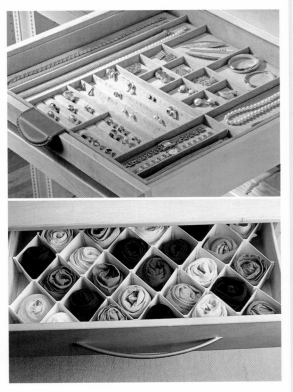

▶ ***ALL HUNG UP***
*This clever hanger keeps scarves accessible and wrinkle free.*

▲ ***THE LITTLE THINGS***
*Drawers are the answer to keeping small items dust free and out of sight. Drawer dividers come in all shapes, sizes, and materials, from cardboard to canvas.*

# hers 'n' his

No matter how harmonious the relationship, many couples find sharing a clothes closet to be a tug-of-war. She needs a high rod for dresses, while he needs a place for neckties; he's got four pairs of shoes, she's got 15. Different storage needs clearly call for different closet components. Glean ideas for blissful cohabitation from these separate but proximate closets. If sharing a single closet is your only option, consider dividing the limited space with an RTA shelf system—how you divide *that* is up to you.

**(ALMOST) IDENTICAL TWINS** At first glance the matching closets on this page seem like mirror images, each with a storage tower on one side and clothes rods on the other. But look again. On the right, he gets upper and lower hanging rods for jackets, shirts, and pants, plus drawers for underwear, socks, and t-shirts. Shoes and accessories require minimal space, so there's room for his shoe-care kit and a favorite board game (below). On the left, she gets cubbies to hold 24 pairs of shoes, space to hang longer garments, and shelves for folded tops and sweaters. Her undergarments and accessories occupy the chest of drawers between the closets. A hook on her door is a handy spot for a hat and bag.

## quick tip

For an instantly neat look, use matching hangers. Simply replacing a hodgepodge of wire, plastic, and wooden hangers with a single type can make a big difference.

**SIDE BY SIDE** This pair of closets originally had sliding doors that always obscured half of each closet's contents. The new French doors add a stylish touch in addition to making the closet more accessible. Gauzy curtains gathered onto top and bottom rods hide contents from view when the doors are closed. Custom shelving—arranged differently for his closet and hers—was built from birch plywood, which is sturdy and easy to prime and paint. His section has hooks for belts and plenty of rod length for shirts and folded pants. Her closet (right) has a short rod for long skirts and dresses, and two stacked rods for blouses and pants. A cubby tower stores folded sweaters, shoe boxes, and purses, while the uppermost shelf stows seldom-used items.

# shoe crazy

Sneakers, pumps, oxfords, loafers, and flip-flops—no matter what types of shoes you own, a jumbled pile of them on your closet floor is not a great idea. Shoes can be scratched and crushed, and searching for a matching pair wastes time. Luckily, there are numerous ways to store footwear neatly and attractively. Whatever solution you choose—be it a tilt-out bin, a slanted board with cleats to hook heels on, cubbies, or shelving—make sure it has at least some slots at waist level or higher so that you can easily see and retrieve your shoes. And don't forget to include room for future acquisitions.

Freestanding slanted racks offer open storage; these work best for shoes with heels, as flat-heeled shoes may slide off. Shelves and cubbies

▲ **SNEAKER KEEPER**
*Tiered metal racks allow air to circulate around damp footwear. A wicker basket serves as a temporary hamper for socks.*

are usually the best option for boots. If shelf space is limited, consider a metal rack or a pocketed plastic, mesh, or canvas shoe bag that hangs over the door or from a clothing rod.

To keep shoes dust free, stack them in plastic, cardboard, or canvas boxes. Use labels or clear plastic boxes so you can review your collection at a glance—or glue a snapshot of the pair to one end of the box. Maintain the shape of your favorite footwear with cedar or plastic shoe trees for leather shoes, crumpled tissue paper for cloth ones, or boot shapers. To keep shoes smelling fresh, tuck in fabric-softener sheets; replace monthly.

◀ **MADE TO ORDER**
*This bedroom closet is a mini–shoe salon. To replicate this look using an RTA unit, add facing and crown molding.*

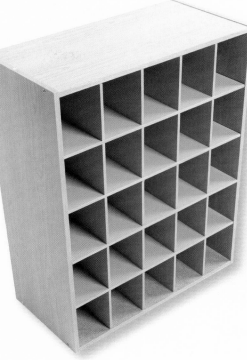

### ◀ CUBBIES

One of the most popular ways to store shoes is to slot them in cubbies (left), which come in lots of sizes and finishes. Some units can be stacked or added on to if necessary. Hanging canvas ones are a flexible choice, since they can be collapsed and moved easily.

### ▶ HANG-UPS

Slip the metal shoe rack at right over the closet door, and you're set. Vinyl-coated prongs protect the insides of shoes and position each pair for easy viewing. For a softer look, try a pocket shoe holder like the zinnia-pattern one at far right.

# walk right in

A spacious walk-in closet with a dressing area and vanity seating is, for many, the ultimate luxury. But it doesn't matter how big or small your walk-in closet is if you can't actually walk into it. Clear out the clutter and check out these fine examples of functional and efficient walk-in closets.

**WARDROBE WALL** A freestanding wardrobe or built-in storage unit can convert an otherwise empty hallway into a spacious walk-in closet. The elegant example below combines rods and shelving with closed cupboard and drawer storage for a tidy, unified look. Handsome molding and raised paneling echoes the home's vintage architecture; the decorative glass doors add even more visual interest while shielding clothes from direct sunlight, which can cause fading.

**NEAT RETREAT** Flooded with light, the airy closet above is really a dressing room unto itself. Its custom cabinetry offers drawers galore and open shelving for folded clothes. Adjacent, a column of narrower shelves displays handbags, a jewelry box, and assorted items. A long countertop by the window serves as a vanity. Out of view on the wall opposite the window is plentiful hanging space for clothing as well as shoe storage.

## quick tip

Natural light is an asset when coordinating colors for the day's outfit. It may save you from realizing too late that those "black" socks you chose were really navy. Direct sunlight, however, can fade dark fabrics, which is why you should limit light on your wardrobe from windows and skylights.

**A PLACE FOR EVERYTHING** This large walk-in has it all. Hanging clothes and shoes (left) are categorized by formal, casual, and business attire. Bins on high shelves hold out-of-season garments. In the back of the closet above, a drawer-and-shelf unit stores folded sweaters and displays jewelry boxes. A pair of lamps illuminates the space. The bench provides a convenient surface for staging the day's outfit, packing a suitcase, or gathering items to be taken out of the closet.

# the well-appointed male

Although many of the closets in this book work equally well for both men and women, the ones pictured here are expressly designed for the stylish storage of guy's clothing—including ties, belts, and suits. Rich wood cabinetry suggests a classic men's-club aesthetic, which can be skillfully combined with contemporary practicality to address specific storage needs, such as racks for neckties and tailor-made hanging compartments.

CRAFTSMAN ELEGANCE The built-in wood cabinetry, granite countertops, and window seat of this roomy walk-in closet are finely crafted to match details throughout the rest of the house. Custom retractable necktie racks flank the decorative window; such one-of-a-kind details are hallmarks of professionally designed luxury closets.

Many staples of the male wardrobe require special storage solutions. Neckties and belts can be rolled up and stashed in divided drawers or hung up in full view. Beyond the traditional hanger, slacks storage options include roll-out racks and pull-out rods.

◄ **SLICK SLACKS**

*Glide-out pant racks are a feature available with various closet systems. Here, an entire row of slacks pulls out; rubber rings on each rod prevent garments from slipping onto the floor.*

◄ **TIE CADDY**

*Hang ties on carousels like this motorized one, which features a light to help you see colors and patterns. Some plug into wall outlets; others run on batteries.*

◄ **TIE DRAWER**

*Closet companies offer specially designed drawers for neckties, which stay neat when rolled and tucked into individual compartments.*

**COMPACT AND COZY** There's a lot of room for clothes in this tight space. A tall cabinet topped with crown molding features both shelves and rods. Socks and underwear reside in an antique burled-wood bureau. Wall racks hold ties and belts. Recessed lights illuminate jackets and slacks, which are hung at full length to fight wrinkles.

**HIS CORNER** This closet features rich wood tones and a bench containing storage underneath. Multiple rods, drawers, and shelves keep clothes wrinkle free. Recessed halogen spotlights shine brightly into all areas of the closet, making it easy to locate clothes and match colors. A dedicated nook keeps a briefcase at the ready.

# learning from the pros

When you're planning a closet, you can pick up some pointers by taking a look at luxurious closets designed by professionals. Even if the final product—like the one shown on these pages—is out of your price range, you can reap great ideas to apply to your own project.

Most important is a layout that maximizes space and places your belongings in easy-to-access spots. The first part of this book offered tips and examples for creating a good closet layout. Making a scale drawing of your closet according to the measurements you've taken is helpful. Lay sheets of tracing paper over your initial sketch so you can play around with various designs until you come up with just the right one. (In fact, that's how many professional designers do it.) Or look into software specially designed to help you create a closet plan.

Many professional designers and closet-design companies offer all the bells and whistles: pull-out shelves, glass-fronted cabinets, tilt-out bins, pull-down ironing boards, and gliding or rotating racks for belts and ties. You can purchase many of these same features for your own closet from home-improvement and organizing stores. (See examples of components pictured throughout this book, and consult the Resource Guide on pages 124–125 for suggestions.)

### WHOM TO HIRE

In the small world of closet design, professionals may be interior designers, specialized closet designers, or professional organizers who redesign closets as part of a more general organizing program. Some, but not all, belong to the American Society of Interior Designers or to the National Association of Professional Organizers. Interior designers and closet designers will visit your home to assess your space and belongings, draw up a

plan, and hire a carpenter to install it. A professional organizer usually works a bit differently. After assessing your space, the organizer will come up with a plan that might incorporate a prefab system available on the Internet or components from a home center, to be installed by a handyman or carpenter.

Specialized closet-design companies offer comprehensive built-in systems, providing design, components, and installation in one package. A company representative measures your space and gives you an estimate based on a design that is specific to your closet. Once you sign a contract, the company delivers the components and sends an installer to put it all together.

### CASE STUDY

This large walk-in closet/dressing room was custom built by a master cabinetmaker to take advantage of every inch of a long, rectangular space created by a room addition. Maple cabinetry inlaid with ebony gives the space a warmth and style rarely found in closets. Light is abundant, both from a skylight and from recessed downlights in the ceiling.

Looking from the back of the closet toward the entry (left), you see open compartments for hanging clothes, each featuring a hook for the next day's outfit or garments to be ironed. (One cabinet houses a pull-down ironing board.) Below the rods, drawers and shelves make maximum use of space.

At the back of the closet (above), a three-way mirror dominates. On the right, tall cabinets store longer and special-occasion attire; shelves hold accessories and out-of-season wear. Drawers stow sweaters, socks, rolled belts, and so forth. At each end of the closet, a dream of a shoe cabinet has a glass front for visibility (as do some of the drawers). Acrylic shelves show off shoes.

# taming a teen closet

As your child becomes a teen, his or her closet needs to keep up. Wardrobes are likely to be expanding and interests changing. Fortunately there are all sorts of bright and appealing organizing accessories available to help transform your child's closet into an attractive and usable space for a growing teenager. Involve your teens in the planning process, and they might actually want to put their stuff away!

**BEFORE** This teenage girl's closet was a terror, crammed with a single bowed rod and shelf to hold everything. The existing bifold door was the only plus, giving full access to the closet's contents. The *Smart Closet Makeovers* team began by removing outgrown and out-of-style clothes to make room for the good stuff.

**AFTER** Selecting a coated-wire system allowed the team to approach this makeover as an inexpensive do-it-yourself project. Once the closet had been measured and the components acquired at a home organizing store, putting it all together took just a few hours. Two rods mounted at different heights took care of the hanging clothes. On the left, a wire-drawer unit stores folded sweaters, tops, and accessories—clear plastic liners prevent the wire from making indentations on clothing. On the floor, a basket keeps laundry in check.

**THE DETAILS** Sometimes it's the simple things that pull a closet together. In this case, matching plastic bins with lids contain folded clothes and shoes. The rest of the teen's clothing is now on matched wooden hangers—another way to visually tame a closet.

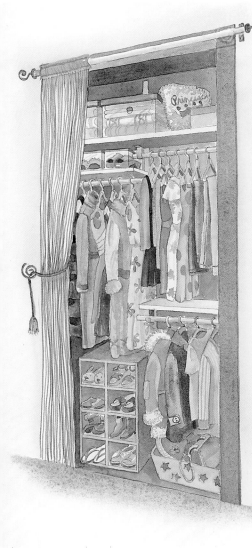

### CLOSET SKETCHBOOK

Teens' closets should reflect the individuality of their owners. Here are two alternatives for organizing the closet shown on the facing page. In the sketch above, the bifold door opens to reveal a cool locker-style dresser that matches a similar piece just outside the closet. Shelving above the dresser holds handbags and shoes in clear acrylic boxes. Two stacked rods handle hanging items. In the design at left, the door has been replaced by a jaunty striped drape. A third rod accommodates more hanging clothes; shoes are now in cubbies.

# a touch of whimsy

For kids' closets, choose a flexible system that can effortlessly accommodate changing wardrobes and gear as your child grows. On the outside, get creative with door decor to perk up the whole room. Bins and boxes, pegs and hooks, hanging shoe pockets, and colorful mesh bags can hold everything from shoes to dolls.

**FLEXIBLE SPACE** Typically, young boys have few hanging clothes. In the closet below, a pair of kid-height rods, plus a third that's higher up, do the job, while much-needed shelving takes care of everything else, from books to toys

**ARTFUL FANTASY** Creative paint effects transported the child's room and closet below to storybook country, complete with grassy hills, a blue sky, and a cobblestone path. Cottage-style doors open to reveal a spacious closet with double rods for a collection of tiny outfits. The rods are spaced far enough apart to support larger clothes as the child grows. There's also room to add shelves, bins, and other storage accessories.

to baseball caps. Pull-out wire bins catch odd-shaped sports equipment for easy cleanup. When the boy becomes a teenager, the same shelves can house new gear—trophies, video games, music CDs, and school supplies.

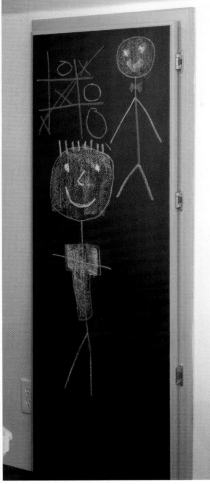

**CHALK IT UP** This black closet door is also a writing surface. It's sealed with several coats of chalkboard paint, available at hobby shops and art-supply stores.

## quick tip

If a young child has lots of clothes to hang, stack rods two or three high by suspending rod doublers from the top rod. That way, you need devote only a small amount of horizontal space to hanging clothes, leaving the rest for more versatile shelving and drawers. As the child grows, rearrange the rods to suit his or her needs. (Turn to page 11 for recommended heights.)

**SLAM DUNK** Sliding closet doors can become your canvas. The cleverly painted locker design below sets a playful tone for an aspiring athlete's room; the raised paneling gives a realistic three-dimensional quality to the "lockers." Behind the doors is a roomy closet that stores everything from clothes to sports equipment.

# for the youngest set

Versatile cubbies, stacking cubes, and shelves with dividers make rearranging closets painless as kids grow. Shoe cubbies may start out holding folded stacks of toddlers' tiny pants and t-shirts or a collection of toy cars, then graduate to storing sneakers and cleats as originally intended. Cubes might house a zoo of stuffed animals now, backpacks or purses later.

**NURSERY IN STEREO** Twin girls share the pretty room below and its wide-open closet framed by sheer, fringed curtains. Below a display of no-longer-used bassinets, a long shelf shows off a parade of dainty hats. Two rows of rods hold most of the girls' outfits now, while dresser drawers will accommodate more clothes later on. The shelves stow shoes, piggy banks, books, and even bedding.

**CRAYON BRIGHT** A cheery sight greets the lucky child who opens the door of this closet (above). The clothes themselves are part of the display: special-occasion dresses in rainbow hues face outward on a high rod. Overalls, hats, and a friendly folded quilt add more color to the mix. A ladder allows access to the upper reaches when Mom or Dad is around to supervise.

## quick tip

Add dividers or a set of bins, boxes, or baskets to keep open shelves tidy. For toys, art supplies, and kids' collectibles, choose small containers rather than large ones so items don't get buried. Unless you use clear containers, identify contents in large letters or use a picture of what's inside as the label.

Because infants' clothing and belongings are as teeny as they are, and their wardrobes are typically not as extensive as those of older children, an armoire can be a perfect storage solution. When the child's belongings have outgrown the enclosed space, you'll have a versatile piece of furniture that can house toys and games—or be put to other uses entirely.

The armoires pictured here were designed especially for children's rooms. They feature drawers for folded clothes and bedding as well as rods for hanging garments and shelves for knickknacks.

For babies and toddlers, one short rod is sufficient for extra-special dresses or coats, or for slightly larger-size clothes that your child will soon grow into. Stack colorful baskets and bins on the shelves for toys and other small items.

In armoires as well as closets, don't overlook the doors. The insides of armoire doors are handy places for decorative hooks, blackboards, or bulletin boards on which kids can create or hang their artistic masterpieces. Up top, you can use the armoire's roof to put special toys and other keepsakes on display.

# creativity center

Do you love putting together inventive scrapbooks, sewing eye-catching quilts, or knitting colorful scarves? Perhaps your creativity finds its outlet in wrapping distinctive packages for loved ones, or designing one-of-a-kind greeting cards. Whatever your hobby, you need space to stash all those wonderful supplies you just can't resist adding to your crafting collection. Instead of clearing works-in-progress off the dining-room table every night, turn a spare closet into a crafts closet.

## THE MAKEOVER

OBJECTIVE
- **Transform a guest closet into a crafts center**

IMPROVEMENTS
- **Removed clothing rod**
- **Installed shelving**
- **Added curtain rods for wrapping paper and ribbon**
- **Built fold-down table**

**AFTER** With a closet dedicated to crafting and wrapping, supplies and projects no longer clutter up living spaces. Yet it's all right here, tucked neatly inside, ready to go. In addition, materials that had been scattered all over the house are now in one place where they're easy to find and use. Displaying items such as colorful scrapbook papers and ribbons—attractive in and of themselves—inspires creativity and reveals all the raw materials available for a given project.

**BEFORE** Overflow from a bedroom closet had spilled into the guest-room closet above—it was time for a trip to Goodwill. Coincidentally, the tenant in this apartment need-ed a place to store scrapbooking and gift-wrapping supplies, as well as a work center for both activities. Putting two and two together, the *Smart Closet Makeovers* team had its answer: repurpose the guest-room closet.

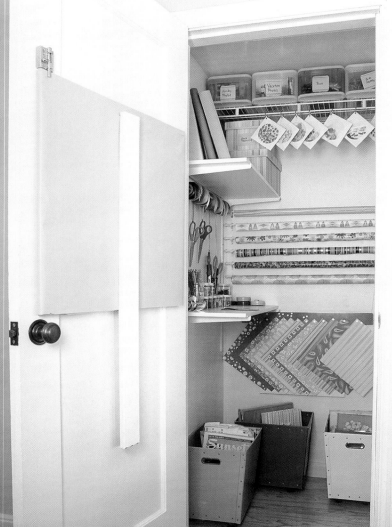

**DECORATIVE STORAGE** The closet rod was removed to make room for new shelving on either side. The existing coated-wire shelf now holds labeled plastic boxes filled with photos. Assorted stickers, cleverly stored in CD sleeves, hang from clip-on key rings. Striped fabric-covered boxes store less-often used gift-wrapping and crafts items, as well as more photos.

**FOLD-DOWN TABLE** To create a second work surface, the team attached a pull-down shelf to the inside of the closet door (above right). It's perfect for working while standing up or seated on a tall rolling stool that can be stored inside the closet. Made of $\frac{1}{2}$-inch plywood covered with self-adhesive paper, the shelf is attached with hinges to the door; a 1-by-3-inch support post folds up when not in use. Rubber on the post's end protects the floor when the table is open. A sliding bolt (shown on facing page) secures the table against the door when it is closed.

**TASK AREA** Hanging items rather than stashing them in drawers or boxes makes them accessible and decorative, too. The team installed a slender metal curtain rod below the top left shelf to hold rolls of bright ribbon. Scissors attach with easily untied loops of ribbon. Curtain rods on the right dispense wrapping paper; now it's a cinch to unroll a length of paper and cut it to size. A solid melamine shelf serves as a mini workstation. Glass jars contain an inspiring collection of stickers, gift tags, glitter, and other supplies.

# project headquarters

Whether you have an entire closet at your disposal to dedicate to supplies or just a nook borrowed from a corner of a room, you can make it an efficient and accessible craft center by using a little imagination and employing some basic organizing components. The inspiring crafts closets on this page can help you get started.

**SCRAPBOOKING CENTRAL** The addition of shelving on three sides turned the small closet above into a center for scrapbooking materials, office supplies, and even reference books. Metal brackets support the shelves on the back wall; a special bracket used for the top shelf also holds a clothes rod, which carries clips and S-hooks for scissors and tools. The shelves on the right are supported by cleats (for more information, turn to page 80).

**QUILTER'S HEAVEN** Quilting and sewing enthusiasts know that a fabric collection can quickly grow to alarming proportions. The deep closet at left has been transformed into the ultimate personal fabric shop for an avid seamstress with a home-based quilt-making business. With careful planning, you can use a roomy closet as the center for almost any kind of business you operate from home.

# the organized crafter

Ready to dream up a crafts closet of your own? Consider lining your closet walls with cork tiles, pegboard, or fabric-covered foam core to create surfaces for hanging everything from baskets of quilting thread or colored pencils to decorative paper and stickers.

To create a work surface, you could install a hinged pull-down table like the one on page 44, or build a fixed shelf out of painted plywood mounted with standard brackets (for more about bracket choices, turn to page 82).

One of the organized crafter's favorite tricks is to appropriate ordinary household items for storing supplies. Silverware caddies are terrific for paintbrushes, crayons, or pens. Put curtain rods, paper-towel holders, and bath-towel racks to work holding spools of ribbon or tubes of wrapping paper for holidays and other occasions.

▲ **NICE THREADS**
*Drawer organizers intended for everything from spice jars to silverware can be a boon to crafters and sewing enthusiasts.*

▲ **PRESERVING MEMORIES**
*Choose only archival-quality scrapbooks for your cherished collections, be they photos, vintage postcards, or menus from favorite restaurants.*

◀ **GOTTA LOVE THAT PEGBOARD**
*Borrowing from the workshop idea of hooking tools on pegboard, this wall-mounted organizer keeps thread, needles, scissors, and other sewing necessities orderly and easy to find. You can choose from among many accessories for hanging; here, a standard spool holder and a small bin do the work.*

◀ **HAVE PAPER, WILL TRAVEL**
*A wheeled cart can be packed with supplies and then rolled out of the closet when it's time to get down to business. The top of the cart shown here has a sturdy work surface. This cart was specially designed to hold gift wrap, but you could also adapt a rolling kitchen cart. To customize a cart that has doors, add bins or baskets inside.*

# office/guest room

Converting a closet into a home office or an office-supply center is easy: simply borrow space from a closet in a guest room, a hallway, or even the living room. Whether you add a desk or just a cabinet and a few shelves, you'll feel better organized and in control. Because an office closet is almost always multiuse, choose your doors wisely. Bifold doors take up the least amount of space when open, but swing-out doors offer vertical surfaces for bulletin boards and chalkboards. Or take off the doors entirely so that your closet office is an integral part of the room.

## THE MAKEOVER

### OBJECTIVE

- **Redesign for multipurpose storage**

### IMPROVEMENTS

- **Cleared closet of unneeded, little-used items**
- **Organized files and supplies**
- **Created space for guests' belongings**
- **Added large filing cabinet**

**BEFORE** Multipurpose storage was the goal for this combination guest room and home office. The closet needed to accommodate guest linens and the owners' extra clothing, plus files, books, and papers. To begin, the *Smart Closet Makeovers* team moved the old wooden trunk to the basement, distributed some of the clothing to other closets, and sold an unused computer. A house-wide scavenger hunt turned up files and papers in other locations; these were merged with the ones in this closet to create a central spot for documents.

**AFTER** This closet is equally guest- and office-friendly. The key to organizing the office items is a new four-drawer file cabinet (left) for personal and professional records; a flip-open compartment contains binders filled with invoices and expense records. A magnetic board displays to-do lists front and center. The shelves to the left of the cabinet hold periodicals and reference books; up on top, labeled document boxes contain office supplies. For guests, there's room at the right to hang clothing, a shelf overhead for blankets, and another shelf to the left for guest linens, a stash of reading material, sightseeing guides, and toiletries (see detail above). Below, rolling bins collect paper for recycling. The team chose coordinating turquoise and red boxes, towels, and binders to unify the closet's appearance.

### CLOSET SKETCHBOOK

In an alternate design, the emphasis is on guest-room functions. Where there are fewer papers to store, the large file cabinet isn't needed. Instead, inactive files can go in boxes on the top shelf, active ones in a rolling cart (the bottom shelf has been removed to make room). Periodicals are neatly contained in magazine butlers on the top left shelf, with boxes of office supplies below. That leaves room for hanging pockets to hold guests' shoes, clothing, and even a small storage box or two. Finally, there's room for guests to hang clothes and store luggage; extra bedding is on the top shelf.

# tidy work spaces

To create a fully functional office in a closet, all you really need is a 24-inch-deep space. Add an electrical outlet and you're in business, literally. You can build a desk designed specifically for your closet's dimensions or buy one ready-made. Cabinets, rolling file carts, and modular drawer units can be found in sizes to fit underneath just about any work surface. Shelves for books and office supplies make the most of your closet's vertical space. Finally, don't forget lighting, which can be installed using existing wiring or plugged into an outlet (for more help, turn to page 88).

SECRET STUDY The beauty of the office below is that it's located close to other rooms in the home, yet it can easily be concealed from view. A translucent glass door slides open to reveal a clean arrangement of built-in shelving and cabinets, which capably stow supplies and files. Light-colored wood floors keep the room airy and bright.

**PLANNING NOTES** To create an office in a reach-in closet with a minimum of fuss, start with a stock desktop from a home center or RTA store—sizes range from 20 to 36 inches deep and 28 to 70 inches wide. Add ready-made laminate shelving, or cut and paint the shelves yourself. Use the dimensions at right as a guide.

**CUSTOM CLOSET** Bifold doors open to reveal the beautifully outfitted office closet below, complete with a U-shaped desktop and drawer system that takes advantage of every inch of space. Built-in shelving was specially constructed to accommodate the weight of an extensive book collection. Painting the walls an eye-popping hue helps jump-start creativity.

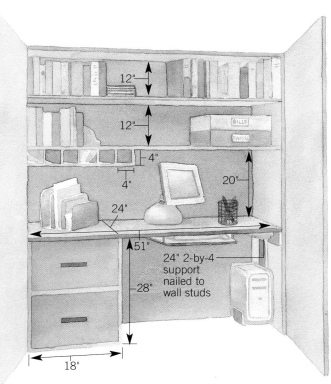

**HOMEWORK CENTER** Adding maple-veneer cabinets and a nearly indestructible laminate desktop transformed the former closet above into an appealing study area for two young brothers. When they grow up, the space can easily morph into an adult's office.

51

# be a media maven

Despite the onetime promise of a paperless computer age, no one can really escape the need to store tax returns, business receipts, and recipe cards, not to mention photos, scrapbooks, and magazines. To avoid having to dig through financial documents every time you want to look at your vacation photos, take the time to organize a portion of a closet so that it's devoted to the storage of your media, papers, and memorabilia.

When dealing with paper, the idea is to file, not pile. Establish clear, logical categories (loan documents, warranties, school papers). Then assign each category to a box or folder, and label, label, label! Select containers—cardboard, plastic, wood, galvanized metal, or wicker—in matching or coordinating colors, but if your papers are valuable, choose acid-free archival products. Individual

▲ **FOR PHOTOS**
*Organizing photos is a pleasure when you slip them into paperboard boxes and albums in coordinating colors. Pair boxes with albums, putting selected prints into the albums and the overshoot and negatives into the boxes.*

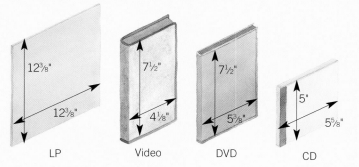

LP — 12³⁄₈" × 12³⁄₈"
Video — 7¹⁄₂" × 4¹⁄₈"
DVD — 7¹⁄₂" × 5³⁄₈"
CD — 5" × 5⁵⁄₈"

▲ **COMMON MEDIA SIZES**
*Use these standard sizes of visual and auditory media to plan your shelving needs.*

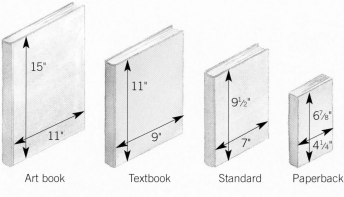

Art book — 15" × 11"
Textbook — 11" × 9"
Standard — 9¹⁄₂" × 7"
Paperback — 6⁷⁄₈" × 4¹⁄₄"

▲ **COMMON BOOK SIZES**
*The drawings above show four common sizes of books.*

documents may be slipped into archival sleeves to protect them further. Avoid putting old papers or photos in plastic boxes or sheets, which may not allow enough air circulation. Archive photos in albums with acid-free pages or in photo boxes, filed by date. Be sure the closet in which you store your valuables maintains an average temperature of 68 to 72 degrees and a humidity of 40 to 60 percent, which rules out most attics and basements.

Audio and visual CDs and DVDs do fine in drawers, on shelves, or in storage containers. Choose containers that are large enough for growing collections. Shelves that hold books must be sturdy and fastened securely into wall studs to carry their weight. When arranging books on shelves, mix standard-sized volumes spine out with larger ones piled flat in short stacks.

▲ **MEDIA-GO-ROUND**

*This brightly painted wooden carousel makes it fun for kids to organize movies and music.*

▲ **OVERSIZE MEDIA**

*Flat files and document boxes are designed for large-format photos, x-rays, maps, and important documents—anything that you want to preserve so edges stay crisp and nothing gets creased or bent.*

▼ **VINTAGE DOCUMENTS**

*Handsome wooden wine-crate filing boxes look good even out of the closet. Flat lids allow you to stack them; cutout handholds make them a cinch to transport.*

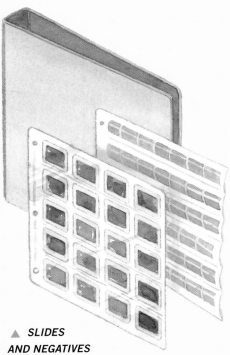

▲ **SLIDES AND NEGATIVES**

*One good way to protect slides and negatives is in slotted plastic sheets. File them by date or subject in three-ring binders and place them on a shelf or in a drawer.*

# snug studies

You can often create a cozy spot for a home office in an unexpected place—a former pantry closet, under the attic eaves, beneath the stairs. Here are some clever closeted offices that appeal to the need for privacy and enclosure. They have the virtue of being close to the action, yet are easily closed off to permit their occupants to get some work done.

UNDERFOOT A clever architect created an under-staircase office in a space that's just over 3 feet wide and 4 feet long. The nook has been wired for a computer and phone; a freestanding desk just fits. Spotlights follow the angle of the stairs. Shelves at the back of the closet (not in view) store videos and books that are used in the adjacent family room.

**SHIPSHAPE** As snug as a skipper's cabin, this office built within a deep closet space feels like a small room. Bathed in light from a skylight, the desktop extends under the shelving on either side. Mixing practical items like books and boxes with beloved photos, art, and collectibles personalizes this homey space so it feels like more than a mere place of work.

**KITCHEN OFFICE** With pocket doors slid back into the walls, a tiny, bright office is easy to access from the kitchen. Matching cabinetry and white tile backsplash give the two spaces visual unity, and generous below-counter cabinet space makes it possible to put away paperwork for a neat look. Textured glass in the transom allows light to stream into the kitchen.

# exercise your options

No matter what kind of closet you're making over, there's always more than one way to do it. Add a shelf here, install a vertical partition there, and you've got a different look. The closet makeover shown here and in the first section of the book is an excellent example of how one space can serve different purposes.

### CLOSET SKETCHBOOK

The guest-room closet on pages 14–15 was revamped by the *Smart Closet Makeovers* team to house everything from clothing to cleaning and office supplies. During the makeover process, the team tried this closet a couple of ways before finally settling on the configuration shown in the photo below. The illustration shows another alternative. In this version, there's more room for clothing; three rods, each with a shelf above, maximize storage options. Office supply and photo storage areas have been shifted to the closet's left side, and bins above hold linens alongside rolled blankets and small luggage. The vacuum and ironing board are still handy, but the wire tower is gone.

## THE MAKEOVER

### OBJECTIVE

- **Create areas for office and craft supplies, photos, clothing, linens, and cleaning supplies**

### IMPROVEMENTS

- **Made space for three rods of clothing**
- **Grouped office, craft, and photo items together**
- **Stowed vacuum and ironing board**
- **Found out-of-the-way space for linens**

# label it or lose it

Once you've assigned your belongings to places in your closets, a labeling system can help keep them there. If you store things in opaque boxes, you'll definitely need labels. For readability, choose labels that are bold and high in contrast. Professional organizers swear by electronic label makers. Handheld models print out whatever you type, in your choice of font and color, laminated and backed with adhesive.

You can also create attractive labels using a computer. Many printers are easily configured for manufacturers' labels—some offer free colorful templates for download from the company site. For pre-readers, try simple graphic representations of socks, shirts, dolls, or blocks. Enhance reading skills of older children with printed labels featuring large letters. Or ask your kids to make their own handwritten labels for a personalized touch.

Affix gummed labels directly onto boxes or shelf edges, or slide cards into label holders. One handsome option for shelf edges is the brass card holder. To attach tags to wicker baskets, clip them with clothespins, tie on gift tags with ribbon, or use key rings with labels.

Don't forget color as a kind of labeling system. Many professional organizers suggest multihued file folders to sort papers. In clothes closets, you could use plastic hangers in several colors—casual clothes on white, business attire on black, formal on red, for example.

◀ **GO CLASSIC**

*Brass label holders add a note of refinement to the edges of shelves in clothes, linen, or pantry closets. Available in stationery stores and online, they screw into the wood for a neat, permanent look.*

▲ **TAG IT**

*Luggage tags find new life as labels for the contents of the baskets seen in the bedroom closet on pages 22–23. You could also use tie-on gift tags the same way.*

▲ **MIX IT UP**

*As this close-up of the crafts-closet makeover on pages 44–45 illustrates, using a variety of labels can add visual punch to your space.*

# my beautiful launderette

The latest trend in laundry rooms is to move them out of the basement or garage and into the house, closer to bedrooms and baths. More often than not, closets—where space is already a challenge—are where these new laundry rooms land. Cleaning products can be stored on shelves or in rolling baskets. Delicates dry well hanging from a clothesline that recoils when not in use, or a drying rack that folds to be stashed away. One space-saving option is a lidded caddy designed to fit between the washer and dryer. You can attach pull-down shelves to the back of the closet door, giving you a place to fold clothes before putting them away.

## THE MAKEOVER

### OBJECTIVES

- **Create a neater, more pleasing appearance**
- **Provide a place to hang drying garments**

### IMPROVEMENTS

- **Added a second shelf**
- **Installed a tension rod for hanging clothes**
- **Used containers to add style and control clutter**

**BEFORE AND AFTER** The roomy laundry closet above had doors that opened wide, allowing most of the space to be used, and was conveniently located near the bedrooms. But it had just one high shelf that was cluttered with an untidy heap of cleaning rags and heavy detergent jugs. The *Smart Closet Makeovers* team added a second easier-to-reach shelf, cut to fit around the vent hose, for detergent, bleach, the iron, and even a dish to catch loose pocket change. Woven boxes on the top shelf contain rags and other items. The team also hid a tension rod inside the doorframe, creating a place to hang delicates to dry.

**TASTEFUL TRASH** Suspended by a ribbon tied to its handles and lined with a plastic bag, a woven box hangs ready to catch dryer lint and trash emptied from pockets.

**NEW USES** Clever containers make for good, clean fun. Here, the team repurposed a bamboo wine caddy to hold spray bottles of stain removers, as well as plain and scented water for ironing. Using containers made from natural materials lends an organic aesthetic to the space.

**GLASS AND FIBER** Glass jars filled with powdered detergent and clothespins brighten up the closet. Woven jute boxes filled with shoe-polishing supplies are labeled using stickers from a crafts store.

# behind closed doors

The washers and dryers shown on these two pages fill the closets in which they are tucked, concealed behind bifold and pivoting doors, cabinetry, and a frosted-glass French door. If you don't have room for the washer and dryer to sit side by side, a stacked system—either a single unit or separate machines designed to be set one on top of the other—is a terrific solution.

**HIDDEN IN THE WALL** This lovely vintage home had one drawback—no laundry room. The solution? A long, wide hallway (left) became the site of a well-camouflaged laundry area. The three lower cabinet doors tilt out to reveal plastic-coated wire hampers. (Open wire sides ensure that damp items won't mildew while waiting to be laundered.) Other cabinets house linens and cleaning supplies. Behind the French door, in what was originally the kitchen pantry, the combination washer/dryer (above) features a pull-out surface for folding laundry. The door was chosen to match others in the house, but the glass panes were sandblasted to hide the closet's utilitarian purpose.

**ALL DRESSED UP** Because it's located in a main living and entertaining area, the stacked washer and dryer at right is concealed behind elegant doors that match those of the wet bar to the left.

**HI-LO EFFICIENCY** Tucked away behind narrow swing doors, single washer/dryer units like the one below are ideal for closets less than 30 inches wide and 35 inches deep.

**CABINET CAMOUFLAGE** Many new washers and dryers, like the ones at right, can be raised off the floor with pedestal drawers—making for easier loading and unloading and providing a place to store laundry supplies. Built-in cabinetry doors slide out and pivot to conceal the appliances. A bonus is the clothing cupboard on the right, complete with rod and shelf, where delicates hang to dry and garments await ironing.

# now you see it...

Even in a home where there's plenty of space for a laundry room, you may still choose to stash washers, dryers, and ironing boards behind closet doors so that the rest of your house feels neat and orderly when it's not wash day.

VOILÀ! An angled pass-through area between a kitchen and a family room is the perfect spot for a full-service laundry center that can be hidden away at a moment's notice. Continuing the design element of wide beadboard paneling, doors in the angled walls swing open to reveal a stacked washer and dryer in one space, a pull-down ironing board with electric socket in another. Abundant light from the ceiling fixture and within the ironing alcove makes every wash day bright.

# for neat freaks

After all that washing and drying, you're not done. There are still socks to match, sheets to fold, and shirts to iron. For dirty laundry or clean clothes that are ready to iron, nothing beats a built-in pull-out bin. A hamper in your clothes closet can serve the same purpose.

A fold-away board can be stored in a wall-mounted cabinet or recessed between studs. Over-the-door racks that hold both iron and board are readily available. Whatever you choose, be sure you have a fireproof surface on which to rest the iron for cooling when you've finished the job.

### ▼ BUILT-IN COMPONENTS

*Pull-out laundry bins come in many materials and designs, but this wicker one (bottom) with a removable canvas insert is a particularly attractive complement to the fine cabinetry that surrounds it. In the same closet system, the ironing board (below) slides back behind a faux drawer front.*

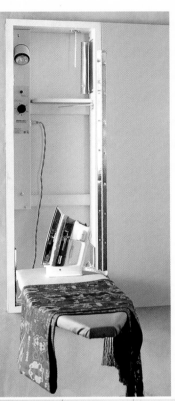

### ◄ PRESSING DUTIES

*This ironing station is mounted between wall studs. Note the timer and the spotlight designed to shut off the power if the iron's left on—a simple, but vital, safety precaution.*

### ▼ ALL IN ONE

*An ironing board that pulls out and pivots plus a sewing table that slides out for quick mending jobs help keep clothing and linens in fine condition.*

# bath towels and bedding

There's something especially satisfying about a closet filled with neat stacks of folded towels and sheets. To arrange your linen closet in the most convenient way, place things that are needed on a daily basis at waist or eye level, with blankets and pillows on the highest shelves. Clip-on shelf dividers will keep stacks from tumbling into one another. If your linen closet must also make room for toiletries, bath tissue, and cleaning products, you can attractively organize them according to function in containers ranging from wicker baskets to old-fashioned tins and glass jars.

**CLOSE AT HAND** Built atop the bathroom counter, the pretty mini-closet above keeps towels neat and dry behind glass. Details such as crown molding, divided-light glass door, and dainty glass doorknob evoke cottage style.

**RUSTIC CHARM** With towels in wicker baskets and toiletries grouped in eye-catching chrome-wire holders, the shelves in this bathroom closet stay organized. Wooden slat shelving allows for air circulation—a good idea in a steamy bathroom.

**CLOSET CLASSIC** Store sheets in sets by size (twin, full, queen, king) and grouped according to room (master, children's, guest). Labeling shelf edges with brass card holders, as shown here, will help maintain order. Or attach paper labels to sheet or towel sets with wooden clothespins. Two alternative ways to keep sheet sets together are to wrap the flat sheet around the folded fitted one and the pillowcases, or to fold both sheets and one pillowcase inside a second pillowcase.

# growing a small room

It's the smallest spaces that require the most ingenuity. In this 300-square-foot studio apartment, the owner, an interior designer, determined that two shallow closets off the apartment's main room could be put to better use as playful design elements that visually expand the room rather than as dull storage areas.

## THE MAKEOVER

### OBJECTIVE

■ Repurpose a cramped clothes closet for more general use in a tiny apartment

### IMPROVEMENTS

■ Relocated clothing
■ Organized media
■ Added a strong design element to the room

**BEFORE AND AFTER** This closet's inefficient and largely inaccessible single clothing rod held barely any clothes. Tote bags were piled on the floor. Now the closet is a stylish mini–media center. A small television and a VCR perch on a dresser containing the clothes once hung from the rod. The classic movie poster and glamorous awning-striped curtains are reason enough to keep the closet door open. Cocktails, anyone?

**DOWN TO BUSINESS** A computer suggests that the fanciful desktop at right is also a serious workplace. Partially concealed behind a curtain to the left side are shelves for books, a scanner, and office supplies.

**WORKING TOGETHER** On the right side of the room, a wide closet has been transformed into a distinctive office/gallery. An antique desk holds papers and a small cache of supplies, as well as artful displays in vintage trophies. On the wall, clippings, swatches, and photos make an eye-catching collage.

# big impact in little spaces

With their doors removed, many small closets can be recast as alcoves or nooks to become extensions of the rooms they adjoin. Bold color and an artful display of objects help two of the spaces on these pages make this transition. For a less decorative closet like the one devoted to pet supplies at far right, keep the door but make the contents attractive to look at when they're on view.

EUROPEAN ALCOVE  This diminutive closet off the dining area had a sloping ceiling and an odd shape, so its usable space was limited. Removing the door, painting the walls, and furnishing the space with a potpourri of dishes, linens, and accessories turned it into a focal point.

CHARDONNAY

**PET CENTRAL**   The former broom closet at right now has everything a furry friend could need. Dog food fills the heavy-duty plastic bin with flip-top lid; hooks keep leashes and collars ready for the next outdoor adventure. A wire bin on the lower shelf holds toys; above, there's space for a jar of treats, shampoo, and medication.

**MINI-LIBRARY**   Inches deep, the closet below was really just a shallow recess in the wall—too narrow even for hangers. The solution: paint the back wall a golden hue, install narrowly spaced shelves, and line them with books. A table lamp offers light for browsing.

## quick tip

Painting the interior of a closet can transform it into a design element that is an integral part of the room. Remove any shelves, prep and prime the walls, and apply a high-quality paint—choose one that is mildew resistant if there's even a hint of dampness in the closet. For uneven or blemished walls, cover with fabric or wallpaper instead of paint.

# dishes on display

In times gone by, every kitchen had its pantry—a narrow room lined with shelves that offered convenient storage for food, dry goods, and dishes. Today, thanks to all the kitchen tools and appliances, specialty cooking ingredients, and decorative dishware that need to go somewhere, pantries are making a comeback. If you have a small closet near your kitchen or dining area, make the most of that space by retrofitting it as a pantry.

**BEFORE** The generous width and handsome double doors of the pantry below were big pluses. But the old composite shelving was sagging under the weight of the dishes, and the contents looked jumbled and crowded. Ho-hum off-white walls did nothing to make the space attractive.

**AFTER** Now the doors stand proudly open to display a butler's pantry closet with major design credentials. The *Smart Closet Makeovers* team replaced the old composite shelves with stronger plywood shelving; instead of four shelves, five were installed, making better use of vertical space. Paint in a Tuscan-inspired hue was applied to create a rich backdrop for dishes and glasses, which have been grouped according to size and type.

## THE MAKEOVER

### OBJECTIVE
- Redesign space for efficiency and beauty

### IMPROVEMENTS
- Replaced sagging shelves, and added an extra one
- Organized dishware and glasses
- Purchased plate rack
- Painted interior

**CLEVER ORGANIZERS** To hold casserole dishes and plates, hoop-style dividers were set over a layer of cushioned shelf liner to keep dish edges chip free. The team attached casters to three wooden wine bins; the two outer bins are used in the upright position while the middle one has been turned on its side to hold rolled-up placemats.

## quick tip

When you store dishes and glassware on open shelving in a pantry, arrange them so that they're attractive to look at *and* easy to reach. The secret is grouping them according to function first, then color, texture, shape, and other characteristics.

**SIMPLE SHELVES** Custom-built shelving is supported by cleats nailed to the wall (for instructions, turn to page 80). On the top two shelves, quarter-round molding attached near the back edge functions as a plate rack for displaying attractive platters.

# a place for everything

Whether you have a walk-in pantry or just a narrow storage space between two studs, the key to making it practical is to group contents according to categories (canned goods, boxed items, glasses, plates), and to make sure every item is in view. A variety of shelf racks and dividers from kitchen and home stores can help.

**IT'S A WRAP** Above, wraparound shelving turns an existing closet into a much-needed pantry with plenty of room for everything from home-canned goodies to cookbooks. Using a glass-front door rather than a solid one makes the tiny kitchen appear larger, allows easy perusal of pantry contents, and lets light pass through.

**CULINARY CUBBY** The small walk-in closet at left became a pantry with the simple addition of shelving. Adjustable oak shelves in a warm golden finish were installed on two sides. Their shallow depth ensures that all items are easily visible. The storage tower at the back features extras such as glass-front drawers for grains and pasta and, above, narrow slots for plates and platters. Storing beans and other dry foods in glass jars is practical and adds a decorative touch.

**BUTLER'S DREAM** In many older homes, butler's pantries were the small rooms or passageways where dry goods, dishes, glassware, and sometimes linens were kept. The updated version at right is chock-full of dishes and glassware, yet it is so well organized that everything is accessible. Glass cake stands, used less often than every-day dishes, occupy the highest shelf. Clip-on wire racks double storage space for cups and small plates. Heavy platters are set on end in a rack placed on the floor beneath the bottom shelf. Country-style touches include a vintage drying rack holding dishtowels, an antique stepladder (handy for reaching that top shelf), and baskets on hooks.

**NO ROOM? NO PROBLEM** If you don't have a closet, consider creating a shallow food pantry between wall studs. Furnished with narrow built-in shelves, it will accommodate a surprising number of spice jars, cans, and bottles. At left, a pantry door that matches the paneling seems to disappear when closed. (For an example of a utility closet created in the same way, turn to page 77.)

## quick tip

If your goal is to store mostly canned goods, pantry shelving can be as shallow as 4 inches. For cereal boxes, make sure your shelves are at least 12 inches deep.

# places for place settings

Whether you use them daily or only for special occasions, your favorite dishes and linens deserve their own storage solution. Eliminate wasted space and opt for organizers such as those shown on these two pages to keep cups, glasses, and dishes in good order. Hooks, hanging racks,

and drawer organizers will help you get more things into less space without crowding. Store linens where they'll stay fresh and wrinkle free, such as in a wide, shallow drawer.

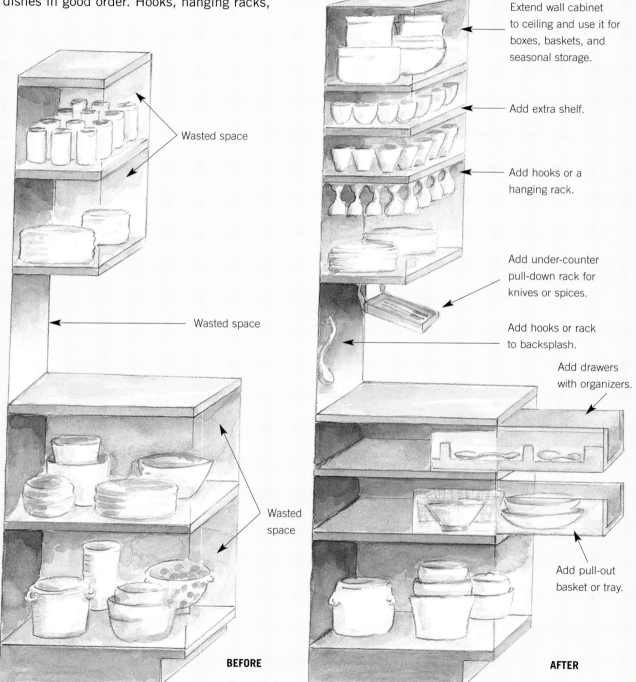

Wasted space

Wasted space

Wasted space

Extend wall cabinet to ceiling and use it for boxes, baskets, and seasonal storage.

Add extra shelf.

Add hooks or a hanging rack.

Add under-counter pull-down rack for knives or spices.

Add hooks or rack to backsplash.

Add drawers with organizers.

Add pull-out basket or tray.

**BEFORE**

**AFTER**

◄ **PAMPERED TREASURES**

Storing fine china calls for special care. Zippered padded containers with built-in separators are a popular solution; choose round ones for plates, divided ones for china cups or stemware. Felt or foam separators, sold at kitchen, linen, and organizing stores, will keep stacked plates scratch free on shelves; paper plates are an inexpensive alternative.

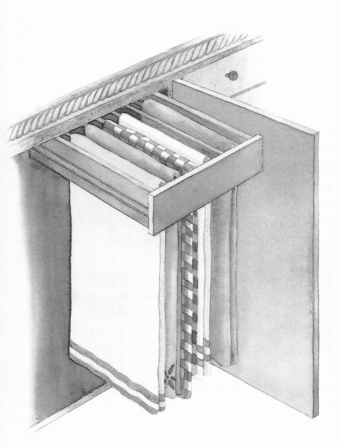

**CRISP LINENS**

Keep your tablecloths, runners, and cloth napkins crisp: hang them or fold and stack them on a shelf or in a drawer where they will have plenty of room. The drawing at left shows linens hanging on large wooden dowels that pull out; this idea could also be adapted using a wall-mounted drying rack or towel bars.

# it's gotta go somewhere

While they're not always pretty, utility closets are essential for stashing all those household necessities: dustpans and brooms, tools, grocery bags, cleaning supplies, and paper goods. The key to keeping it all organized is to compartmentalize. Divide the space horizontally and vertically by using shelves and partitions; melamine and wire systems work equally well for this. Create narrow vertical spaces for an ironing board, mops, and a vacuum cleaner. Assign categories of items to labeled bins or boxes, using small containers like shoebox-size baskets for tools, glues, or lightbulbs.

**MAXIMUM UTILITY** This closet capitalizes on every inch of space, yet its bright and cheery walls help make housework less of a chore. Up on top, a wire shelf is stocked with cleaning supplies and a bucket that has a removable lid and compartments to hold cleansers and tools. A row of hooks and clips on the wall holds everything from extension cords and a dustpan to an apron. A folded step stool leans against the closet's back wall. On the inside of the door, brooms and mops hang from a rack. Clips hold rubber gloves that can be hung after use to drip-dry.

## found space

The often-overlooked space between wall studs is the perfect spot for a shallow broom closet. Studs are usually 16 or 24 inches apart, center to center, so the closet can be about 14 or 22 inches wide—plenty of room for several brooms and mops, and even a small collection of cleaning supplies. The closet below is basically a plywood box. If you are creating a space like this in a garage, you may not want to bother with a door.

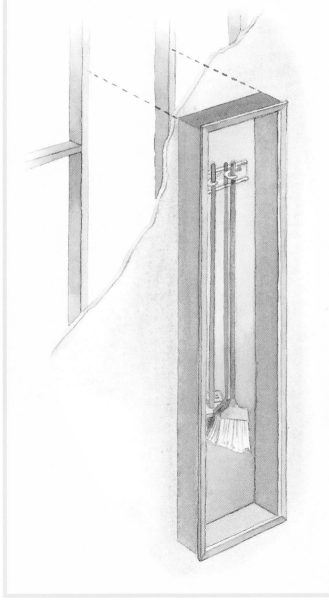

**BROOM CLOSET** Any tall, fairly narrow space in a kitchen or hallway can become a functional utility closet. Hang a broom, a dustpan, and a mop on wall clips and stash a bucket on the floor, close at hand but hidden when the door's closed. You could even mount a paper-towel holder on one wall. Tall, narrow shelves accommodate bottles and cans of cleansers.

basic skills,
cool stuff

WITH A LITTLE KNOW-HOW, a few basic tools, and the right components and accessories, making over a closet can be a satisfying do-it-yourself project. This section of *Smart Closet Makeovers* offers a rich mix of tips, techniques, and products. Step-by-step instructions in the art of putting together closet components share the pages with photos of finished closets and everything that goes into them—from versatile containers for storing all your stuff to light fixtures that brighten the space. First comes a primer on choosing and installing shelves, the basic building blocks of any closet system. Next up are pointers for building ready-to-assemble closet systems and installing lighting fixtures. You'll also learn about options for doors, portable closet systems, and even products for keeping the contents of your closet as fresh as the day you stowed them away.

**PROJECTS AND PRODUCTS**

*Install your own shelving, shop for stylish bins and baskets, and brighten your closet with a brand-new light fixture. There's nothing more satisfying than stepping back to look at your smart new closet and saying, "I did it myself."*

# carry that weight

Shelves—the most basic components in any closet—must be firmly anchored to your closet's walls in order to hold substantial weight. Whether you're building your own shelves or installing shelves as part of a puchased closet system, you can anchor the hardware that supports them in one of two ways. To fasten hardware to the wall studs, use multipurpose screws or wood screws. If you can't position hardware directly over a stud, use the strongest anchor suitable for your wall—shelves designed for displaying photos today might be loaded up with heavy boxes tomorrow.

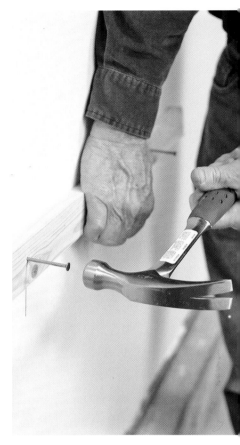

Ceiling joist

16" or 24" on center

Wall stud

**FIND THE STUDS** Wooden 2 by 4s make up the inside framing of most walls, which are usually constructed of wallboard or plaster. If you don't trust the knock-on-the-wall approach to locate the studs that will support your shelves, look for an outlet or a switch, which typically will be anchored to a stud, or check the baseboard, which should be nailed to studs. Or use an electronic stud finder like the one at right, moving it slowly across the wall; it will light up or beep when it passes over a stud. Mark the center of the stud with a pencil and measure out 16 or 24 inches to find the next one. If you're still uncertain, drill exploratory holes in an inconspicuous place. If your home has steel studs, you can locate them in the same way; anchor hardware with sheet-metal screws.

**THE COMMON CLEAT** A cleat is simply a piece of lumber nailed to the wall and into the studs to provide support for your shelf. Attach cleats to support a shelf along its length at the back and at each end. Secure the shelf to the cleat with 6d finish nails or wood screws. A cleat installed at a shelf's end (opposite page) can do more than just support the shelving. Make it do triple duty, holding rod hardware and hooks, too.

## quick tip

A 2-foot carpenter's level is an ideal tool for hanging shelves evenly. Place it against the wall horizontally, crossing a stud, at the height you want the shelf supports. Adjust until the bubble is level, then pencil a line on the wall along the top of the level.

## no studs? no problem

To fasten light-duty shelves in areas between studs or into concrete or brick, use specialty fasteners such as spreading anchors or toggle bolts (in wallboard), or expansion shields (in brick or concrete). As you screw them into the wall, these fasteners expand to establish a firm hold.

◄ ***SPREADING ANCHOR***

*This anchor, also called a molley bolt, has a sleeve that lies flat as it's driven into the wallboard or plaster, then opens against the back of the wall as you screw in the bolt, thus securing it and your hardware firmly in place.*

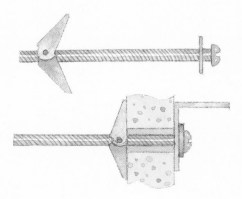

◄ ***TOGGLE BOLT***

*Designed to be anchored into wallboard or plaster, this bolt features wings that open behind the wall. Like a spreading anchor, the bolt gets its strength from being compressed against the wall.*

◄ ***EXPANSION SHIELD***

*Use an expansion shield, also called an expansion bolt, to anchor hardware to a brick or concrete wall. Drill a hole into the wall as wide as the sleeve but slightly deeper. Tap the sleeve in place with a hammer and insert a lag screw; as the screw is tightened, the anchor will expand.*

# simple materials

Although some closet construction calls for solid-wood shelving and fancy hardware, a more economical way to go is to build your own shelves out of common sheet products and support them with ordinary brackets and standards (right).

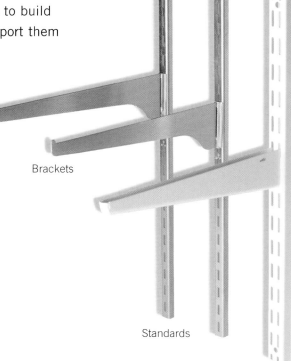

Brackets

Standards

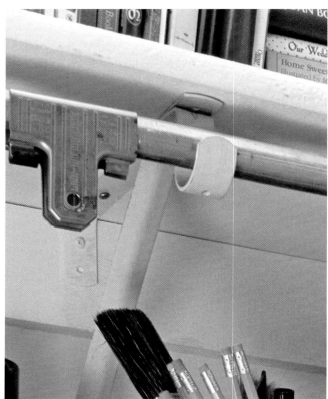

**SHELF SUPPORT** Brackets are the hardware of choice for supporting shelving on a wall. Fixed brackets (right) are screwed directly into the studs, and then the shelves are attached with screws. Made of either wood or metal, brackets come in a variety styles, from utilitarian to highly decorative. Some have specialized uses: for example, the bracket above also has a curved cradle that supports a standard rod below the shelf. Adjustable standard-and-bracket hardware (above right) allows you to tailor a shelving system to fit your needs—and to change the configuration whenever you want. The standards are screwed into studs, and tabs on the bracket ends slip into slots in the standards.

# smoothing rough edges

Some shelving materials have unfinished, rough edges that look better covered. The edges of plywood can be masked by attaching wood trim strips with glue, finishing nails, or both. Melamine and particle board edges can be hidden with veneer tape, as shown below.

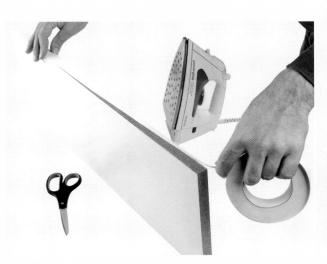

*1.* Use preglued veneer tape, sold at most home improvement centers. Unwind the tape along the edge of the shelf, cut it to length, and press into place with a warm iron following product directions. The tape will be slightly wider than the thickness of the shelf; leave extra on both sides.

*2.* Roll the edging with a veneer roller to flatten the glue and remove air pockets. To finish, run a file, block plane, or razor blade along the overlap on each side to shave the tape even with the shelf faces.

**SHEET SHELVING** *Plywood* is made of thin hardwood or softwood sheets glued together and pressed. Available in several thicknesses and grades, it can be stained to enhance the wood grain, or painted. Because plywood is so strong and durable, you can use it for wide shelf spans. *Particle board*, one of the least expensive options, is made from sawdust and wood chips bonded together with glue or resin, then pressure treated; it's best for short shelf spans, since it tends to warp, sag, and split easily. *MDF* (medium-density fiberboard) is made of wood particles bonded with resin and compressed. It's harder than particle board and takes paint well; look for nontoxic types. *Melamine*, the choice for many closet systems, is particle board laminated with resin. Usually available in white and almond color, it's durable and affordable.

Fir plywood    Oak plywood    Maple plywood    Birch plywood    Medium-density fiberboard    Particle board    Melamine

# off the floor, beautifully

**M**any wire and melamine shelving systems are supported by standards suspended from a wall-anchored horizontal track. While systems may differ slightly, here is how to install the wire type available at most home centers and organizing stores. The track should be anchored to wall studs, but the standards can be fastened to drywall, as shown on page 81.

**1** Position the top of the track on the wall so that as many screw holes as possible are centered on wall studs. Drive a screw into one of the center slots and level the track. After leveling, drive in the rest of the screws.

**2** Lock the first shelf standard onto the track, centered in front of a stud. Use a level to make sure it's hanging plumb and then drive a screw through the center of the standard into the stud. Space standards along the track so they are no more than 24 inches apart and start no more than 4 inches from each end.

**3** Insert the shelf brackets into the standards. Count down the number of slots from the standard tops to be sure the brackets for each shelf are all at the same level.

**4** Lock the shelves onto the shelf brackets, pressing down on them until they snap into place. If your system includes clothing rods, add the supports for them according to the manufacturer's directions.

**5** After determining the shelf standards are plumb, finish screwing them to the wall. Add the caps supplied with the system to the exposed wire shelf ends and to the track as needed.

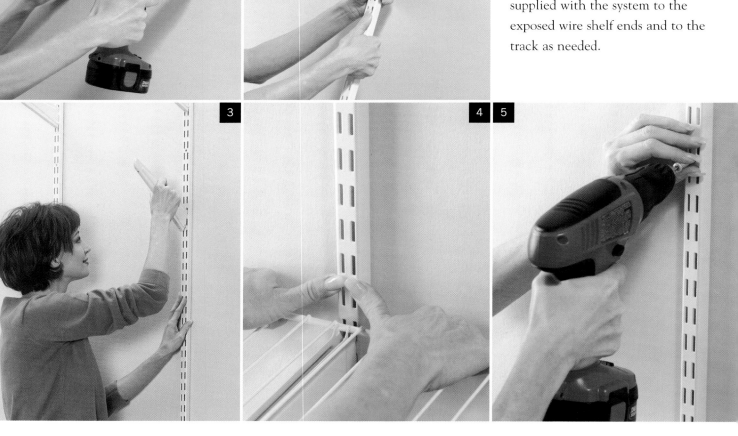

**MIX 'N' MATCH** Handsome melamine shelves and storage units hung from wall-mounted chrome tracks appear to float—making it easy to clean the floor. Modular units allow seemingly endless combinations of shelves, cubbies, and drawers. Heavy units like melamine drawers require tracks and standards to be securely anchored into studs.

# almost-instant wardrobe

Freestanding wardrobes like the ready-to-assemble (RTA) melamine one on the facing page are economical, good-looking, and real lifesavers if you have little or no closet space. And, of course, if you pull up stakes and move, your wardrobe can go right along with you. The same general assembly techniques described below apply to most melamine closet systems. Note that melamine parts are quite heavy and are best assembled right where you plan to use them. Enlist a helper to hold parts together as you work.

**1** Lay out all parts and fasteners; check the instructions that came with your unit to make sure every piece is there. Round up a screwdriver, hammer, and any other tool called for in the directions.

**2** Begin assembling your unit, following the manufacturer's instructions. Most units are put together with a combination of cam studs and locks that fit into prebored holes, as shown; some use regular screws as well.

**3** A special tool like the one shown here may be provided to fasten custom screws.

**4** If screw holes in adjacent pieces don't quite line up, you may need to bore new holes. If things seem a little loose when assembled, an extra screw or some gap-filling polyurethane glue may be needed.

**BEHIND CLOSED DOORS** Its clean design makes this freestanding wardrobe a welcome addition to almost any room. Versatile and portable, it features adjustable shelving and a clothes rod; other styles offer drawers and pull-out pants racks. More elaborate modular RTA units may span an entire wall, providing all the space and convenience of a reach-in closet.

# replacing fixtures

Frustrated with rummaging around for things in your closet's shadowy recesses? It's time to see the light. Even if your closet already has a wired-in ceiling fixture, consider upgrading it with a brighter, more decorative one. Choose a fixture that can provide the illumination you need, but check to make sure it will be in compliance with local building codes (many require lighting fixtures to be 24 inches from all walls and 12 inches from shelving). For energy efficiency, screw in compact fluorescent bulbs to replace incandescent bulbs. Bring your old fixture with you to the store to make sure that the mounting holes of the new fixture correspond to the old ones. You'll also need a pair of wire strippers, a handful of wire nuts, and a screwdriver to install the fixture.

1 Begin by turning off the electrical circuit. Your old fixture will be attached to a housing box. Remove the old fixture, detach its wires (they may be connected with nuts or electrical tape), and check to see if there's a grounding bar (as shown in photo). If not, screw the bar that comes with your new fixture to the housing box. Fasten mounting bolts loosely.

2 If the wires are not already exposed, use a wire stripper to remove ½ to ¾ inch of their insulation. Splice the black fixture wire to the "hot" black circuit wire by twisting them together, and splice the white fixture wire to the incoming white neutral wire. Screw wire nuts clockwise onto the bare ends. Tug at each wire to make sure it's secure. If the fixture has a grounding wire (bare or insulated in green), secure it to the green screw on the grounding bar.

3 Carefully tuck wires into the housing box, keeping the white wire separated from the black one, and secure the canopy to the box. The fixture pictured here has slots that slip over the mounting bolts. Rotate the canopy into place, then tighten the bolts.

4 Screw in the lightbulb and install the globe. The one shown here slips over a threaded rod and is held in place by a decorative nut. Turn the circuit back on at the electrical service panel.

## WARNING

Make sure the circuit you're planning to work on is dead. Test it before making any repairs or connections.

**LIGHTS ON!** A ceiling fixture brightens the entire area of this spacious walk-in closet—especially important if you want to see yourself in the best light when standing in front of a mirror.

# tracks and spots

As an alternative to fixtures that provide ambient light, consider fixtures that illuminate specific areas of your closet. Track lights are one such targeted solution. Tracks can accommodate low-voltage or standard spotlights. While systems differ, the steps below apply to many of them.

**1** Turn off the electrical circuit. This track system has a wire-in connector and a fixture-box saddle that conceals the box and connections. Using wire nuts, splice the connector's black wire to the black circuit wire, the white wire to the white neutral wire, and the green or bare wire to the grounding wire.

**2** Screw the track system's adapter plate to the housing box. While holding the track in position, attach the connector by twisting it onto the track.

**3** If possible, drive screws through the track's mounting slots into ceiling joists. If, however, the joists don't align with the track, use toggle or expansion bolts, as shown on page 81.

**4** Position fixtures along the track as desired; twist them into place. Add any remaining fixture trim—the model shown in the photo includes a saddle that covers the box and the track connector.

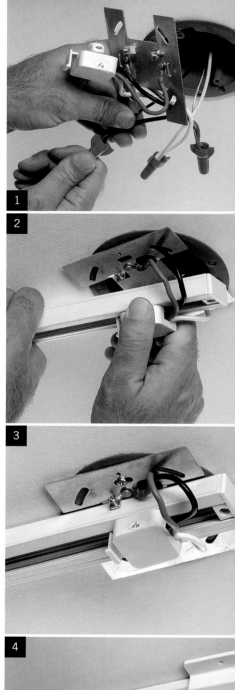

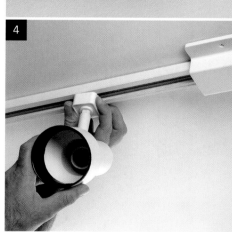

**SWEET SPOTS** Use a spotlight (left) to illuminate a dim corner.

## hiding the source

Various kinds of lights used under kitchen cabinets, in display niches, or below shelving can also brighten your closet. Styles range from low-profile task lights to strip lights (linear bulbs or strings of lights contained in single fixtures). All of these types of lights can be surface-mounted and plugged into an outlet; many can be recessed, and some are battery-powered. Choose from fluorescent, incandescent, or low-voltage halogen or xenon bulbs. Incandescent task lights and some fluorescents are dimmable; xenon and halogen lights have their own transformers, so you can switch them from low to medium to high.

▲ **SUBTLE EFFECTS**

*Tucked behind the shelf molding, low-profile fixtures shed light on rows of slacks and jackets, making it easy to see colors and patterns and giving the closet a warm, inviting appearance.*

▶ **HIDDEN ASSET**

*This halogen strip is battery-operated, so it can go where plug-in lights can't.*

# automatic illumination

For the ultimate in convenience, opt for closet lighting that switches on and off automatically, just like the one in your refrigerator. You'll appreciate not having to change the lightbulb too often because *someone* (that would be you...) forgot to turn it off. Here are a few options.

**MOTION SENSITIVE** Using the same technology that operates motion-detector lights outdoors, the motion-sensor unit shown above screws into an ordinary socket. The light will turn on when you reach or walk into the closet, and will turn off a few minutes after motion stops.

**LIKE MAGIC** If you'd like the closet light to go on automatically when you open the door, you should check out several products that are on the market. The battery-operated light above is affixed to the closet wall. Its sensors are attached to the jamb and the door. Some products take advantage of existing wiring to activate a spring-loaded automatic light switch in the door jamb, much like in a refrigerator. The model shown at right works with both sliding and hinged doors.

**ONE TOUCH** For a super-simple, low-tech solution, buy a battery-operated touch-activated light, available at hardware and home-improvement stores. Mount it on the wall where it's easy to reach, give it a tap, and you've got light.

▲ **LIGHT WELL**

*In this under-stairs home office, a surface-wiring system, color-keyed to the walls, allows for track lighting in an area that wasn't wired for a light fixture.*

Sometimes you can't or would simply prefer not to cut into walls or through the ceiling to route new wiring. In such cases, a surface-wiring system may be the answer. These systems feature protective channels, or strips, and housing boxes that let you mount wiring on practically any wall or ceiling material. The electrical cable runs through the channels, so everything stays neat.

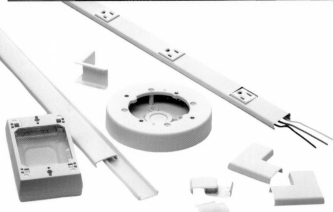

▲ **THE HARDWARE**

*Run wiring in your closet the easy way with a surface-wiring system, available in white, ivory, or black.*

# doors galore

The door may not be the first thing you think of when making over a closet, but it's actually an important element. Different types of doors offer different pluses and minuses. In addition to the examples shown here, look through *Smart Closet Makeovers* for other ideas, like the curtains on pages 22–23 and the decoratively painted doors on pages 40–41.

**IN FULL VIEW** Bifold doors are a neat solution that can be installed to fold back to one or both sides. They provide a full-front opening so you can see and reach everything in the closet. Louvered bifolds have the advantage of allowing air to circulate.

**GLASS GLIDERS** Sliding doors, a standard for many reach-in closets, don't impede the traffic flow of a room. These pantry doors have panels of laminated glass, which resists fingerprints and partially screens the closet's contents. The drawback is that sliding doors allow you to see and reach only one side of the closet at a time.

**GETTING CREATIVE** Shake things up by choosing a door that's not usually intended for a closet. At right, French doors impart a light and airy feel to a pair of closets; curtains look pretty while keeping contents under wraps.

**ON TRACK** A great choice for a casual country-style home, the barn door below slides along a top track. It fits in perfectly with this rustic-feeling bath.

**THE CLASSIC** For reach-in closets, traditional hinged doors (double or single) offer the most storage possibilities because you can mount hooks, overdoor racks and pockets, and other accessories directly to the door. The closet at right features solid wood double doors with raised panels.

# stow it in style

To keep closet contents orderly, choose from boxes with lids, storage cubes, open bins, and zippered containers in all sizes and configurations. You'll find stylish stowaways contructed of plastic, canvas, cardboard, wicker, fabric, or metal. Some come with built-in label holders, while others have windows so you can identify the contents. Many are stackable. Soft, zippered blanket or sweater bags made out of breathable materials provide dust-free storage. For a fun, individual touch, store your stuff in old suitcases, hatboxes, large tins, or other unexpected containers.

▲ **FREESTANDING AND FLEXIBLE**

*This maple veneer cabinet can be used inside the closet or out. The wide bottom drawers slide out conventionally; the cubes have doors. A piece like this can stash everything from socks to shirts to home-office supplies.*

▲ **COLORFUL CUBES**

*Stackable cubes come in many colors and materials; these are notable for their bright striped doors, which swing open at the touch of a finger.*

▶ **VERSATILE BINS**

*Plastic bins in crayon colors look and work equally well in a kid's closet, a mudroom, or a utility closet. This stairstep unit accommodates three sizes.*

 **TOY TOTES**

Baskets made of materials such as willow and wicker come in all shapes and sizes. Choose from flat trays suitable for papers or craft supplies to big cotton-lined bins like these for clothing or toys.

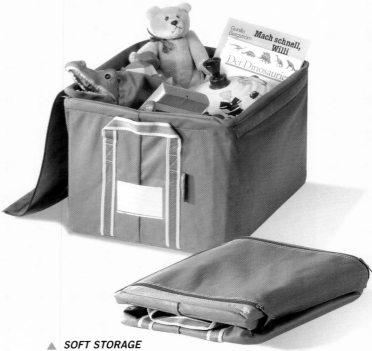

▲ **SOFT STORAGE**

Made of a rugged woven material, this zippered bin collapses flat when not in use but unfolds to roomy proportions to hold toys, blankets, or whatever else needs a home. Handles are a practical feature.

▲ **CANVAS CONTAINMENT**

With its jaunty tropical motif and casual design, this canvas container will perk up closet shelves or sit neatly on the floor to hold odds and ends.

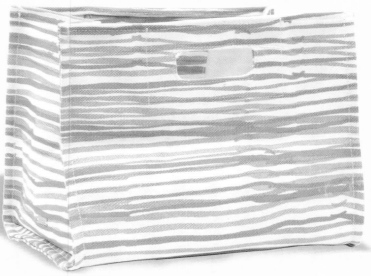

▲ **FILE FASHION**

Made of canvas with a flexible frame, this lightweight bin sits pretty while working hard to organize files.

# low cost, big impact

If you rent and can't alter your closet with built-ins, or you just aren't a do-it-yourselfer, don't despair! You still have plenty of options for transforming your closets, as these organizing alternatives amply demonstrate.

**SOLID SOLUTION** A system like this one gives you the best of both worlds—solid shelving, drawers, and rods that you can easily pack up and move. This aluminum and lacquered steel structure can be placed anywhere, since its adjustable poles are braced between the floor and ceiling. Use it as a room divider, create an instant closet along a wall, or install it inside an empty closet. The basic system offers a variety of shelf and rod configurations; rolling plastic units can tuck in wherever you want or need them.

Invest in flexible organizing pieces like these, and you'll have storage you can use anywhere, anytime. The standing zippered wardrobe and the garment bag store out-of-season clothes or keep your current wardrobe pristine. Hanging shelves of canvas, vinyl, or nylon come in various sizes intended for shoes or sweaters, but you could easily store linens in them, too. Some makers of canvas hanging shelves offer pull-out drawers.

## hang it all

When you're outfitting a closet, consider your vertical options. The more things you can hang, the better. The walls and the back of the door tend to be underused. Put them to work with hooks, overdoor racks, and baskets or bins that attach to the wall. Hang a bulletin or magnet board for memos or even jewelry. Mount large clips for papers or a calendar. Install a wire grid with hooks for belts or scarves, or a towel rack for ties.

▲ **POCKET POWER**

*This clever organizer is useful for holding an array of supplies in any closet in the house. Use it (as shown here) in your office closet to hold pencils, scissors, and such, or in your pantry for coffee filters, kitchen gadgets, or a selection of tea bags.*

▲ **NATURAL BEAUTY**

*Keep a lookout for hanging options that weren't necessarily made for closets. This handsome basket holds anything from toys to towels to laundry.*

◀ **JEWELS**

*Hang this pocket organizer from the rod of your bedroom closet, and every piece of jewelry will be right there on view as you coordinate accessories for the day's outfit.*

# protecting your treasures

Sometimes your prized possessions need more than just the right hanger; they need protection from the elements inside your closet. Among the most common closet pests are moths.

Nontoxic, natural products such as cedar, camphor, rosemary, and lavender have a strong enough odor to deter moths, but their scent—hence their usefulness—lessens over time. In fact, contrary to popular belief, cedar does not kill moths, it just masks the smell of wool, which attracts the insects. Sanding cedar periodically will help release its aroma, but don't store cottons or linens in contact with cedar, as its natural oils may stain them.

Naphthalene mothballs and PDB (paradiclorobenzene) kill both moths and their larvae, but the tradeoff is a strong odor and toxicity from chemicals categorized as carcinogens.

For long-term storage of woolens, feathers, silk, or furs, you'll need to provide additional protection. Before storing such items in sealed bags, boxes, or chests, clean them thoroughly, then air them in the sun for a few hours. If you see any bugs at all, put the article in the freezer for two days, if possible. (Other items that should be stored in sealed containers include books and papers, which can be damaged by silverfish.)

Dampness, which causes mold and mildew to grow, is another closet culprit. Look for garment bags labeled "breathable," and consider using some of the products shown on these pages.

▲ **AROMATIC AND LUXURIOUS**

*This cedar-lined walk-in closet offers the ultimate in storage. The wood's scent naturally repels insects, and its warm tones and rich grain are beautiful to behold.*

### ▲ SCENT OF CEDAR

*You can find cedar shelf liners, blocks, and "mothballs," as well as these rings designed to fit over closet rods. Instead of sanding cedar to release its odor, try a product that sprays on cedar oil.*

### ▲ HANG-UPS

*The silica gel inside this slim dehumidifier absorbs excess moisture, keeping your clothing fresh and odor-free. A signal alerts you when it's time to refresh it in the sunlight for reuse.*

### ▲ KEEPING FRESH

*This battery-operated air purifier neutralizes odors by emitting ozone-rich air; its statically charged metal rods attract pollen and dust.*

### ▲ GARDEN VARIETIES

*Sachets come in all colors and designs; these flower-topped fabric versions are pretty enough to give as gifts and will lend charm and a sweet scent to any drawer.*

# 44 more organizing ideas

**2** **HAT TRICK** In an entryway, a cluster of straw hats makes a design statement. Grouping objects that are alike in function, material, or color enhances their impact.

ONCE YOU'VE REDONE YOUR CLOSETS, you can use your new-found organizing expertise to whip the rest of your house into shape. In the process of emptying your closets, you've probably unearthed a cache of stuff that needs a new home. Or maybe you've cast a discerning eye on various drawers and cabinets and decided that now is the time to tackle them. This is a perfect opportunity to apply the principles you have learned to other nooks and crannies—from your bathroom to your home entertainment center. On the following pages, you'll find 44 more great ideas for bringing order to every room in the house, as well as your backyard. Some of these ideas will help you discover storage space where you didn't think it existed; others help you make better use of the space that's already there. So go ahead and browse through these pages, and then get organized!

**1** **WHITE ROOM** When the things you need to store look this good, why not put them out for all to see? In this all-white kitchen, dishes and glassware in daily use are easy to grab from open shelves.

# packing the pantry

When you're organizing a pantry closet or kitchen cabinet, you needn't rely solely on shelving. There's an amazing array of organizers that you can purchase (either along with new cabinetry or as items you install yourself) to double or even triple your storage space. Cabinets and closets can be retrofitted with pull-out drawers, fold-out inserts, shelf doublers, and back-of-the-door accessories. Shop for these products from kitchen and bath dealers and in home centers, organizing stores, and online catalogs.

3

4

**3 STEP UP** Get the most out of your shelf space with risers and tiered racks that raise a second and third row of items into view. Use them in the kitchen for canned goods, spices, and condiments, in the bathroom for toiletries, or in a curio cabinet for showcasing favorite collectibles.

**4 CULINARY CABINET** Open this fold-out cabinet insert and you'll find a relatively small space packed with an astonishing amount of canned food, boxes, and bottles. Pivoting metal racks allow access to everything, with enough space left over for racks on the doors.

**7** **QUICK ADD-ON** Sometimes the simplest solutions are the best. A sleek metal rack hooked over the top of a closet door provides just enough extra space for snacks, condiments, and cooking ingredients that would otherwise crowd cupboard shelves.

**5** **FOUND SPACE** A shallow niche in a remodeled kitchen displays spices, tea, and home-canned preserves, and it looks good, too. Stealing space like this is a great way to expand your storage possibilities.

**6** **SLIDING SHELVES** Replacing stationary shelves with drawers on full-extension slides makes it a breeze to reach items way in the back. This upgrade is available from most cabinet dealers, or you can order roll-out shelves that attach to existing ones from a kitchen supply catalog. Drawer guides support up to 75 pounds, so you need not worry about overloading your shelves. In this kitchen, the message board on the inside of the door is a handy place for notes and coupons.

# beyond spice racks

When it's easy to see and reach spices and condiments, you're more likely to use them—and that makes for more inspired cooking. On these pages you'll find simple but effective storage ideas for all those little bottles and jars. Some make use of pull-out inserts that come with new cabinetry, others can be purchased separately. Keep in mind that well-placed shelves can go a long way toward organizing your cooking ingredients, too.

8

9

**8 IN AND OUT** Just inches wide, this cabinet provides shallow storage for spices, baking supplies, and condiments. This design can also be used for mixers in a wet bar or for shampoo, lotions, and after-shave in the bath.

**9 TUCKED AWAY** Especially helpful in kitchens that have more drawers than cabinet space, a tiered insert in the second drawer from the top helps spices stay fresh by keeping them out of the light (you can use this trick for teas and cake-decorating supplies, too). These inserts can be trimmed with a table saw to fit most drawers. In the deep drawer below, a lateral divider keeps taller bottles and jars upright.

**10** **WITHIN REACH** A little creativity can turn a commonly overlooked corner into an efficient storage space. A vertical pullout next to the stove puts condiments and spices close at hand for a busy cook.

**11** **IN PLAIN SIGHT** When cabinet space is tight, position ingredients where they can be seen and reached. A commercial-style metal shelf displays spices on risers and could also accommodate cookbooks or decorative items; utensils and saucepans hang by S-hooks. More risers keep the rest of the spice collection in view at the back of the cooktop.

# clean and serene

Reducing visual clutter in your bathroom can help you create both a stylish look and a soothing atmosphere. In keeping with that principle, here are a few ways to store towels and supplies. Some are built in, requiring the skills of a capable carpenter. Others are nearly instant, the sorts of projects that any aspiring do-it-yourselfer could easily tackle. All work well in roomy and space-shy bathrooms alike.

**12** USE EVERY INCH This easy-to-install étagère isn't a new idea, but it's one that has endured. So practical and simple, it makes excellent use of otherwise wasted space. You can find this type of freestanding cabinet in many bath and home stores.

**13** THE UNFITTED LOOK Many bathrooms feature freestanding or unfitted vanities that have the look of traditional furniture. Here, a central storage tower provides a stylish home for towels and bath supplies. Additional drawers are mounted above each sink for toiletries.

**16** VIVE LA FRANCE! An exuberant dash of Old World style conjures up images of sun and sand. Even a set of towels, artfully displayed, can set the tone for a room's decor. The tall baskets on the bottom shelf are useful for storing clean towels or tossing used ones.

**14** ON A ROLL Rolled bath towels cradled in hanging wall racks make an attractive display. On shelves in a conventional linen closet, vary the look by storing large rolled towels, ends facing out, between stacks of folded items.

**15** TINY SPACES ADD UP In this light-filled bath, a narrow column of space at the end of the vanity is put to good use for storing a stack of fresh towels right where they're needed.

# storage down under

When you're looking for extra storage space, anywhere is fair game. Two seldom-used spots are behind cabinet bases and under beds. Think of things you can store flat—placemats, artwork, folded linens, photo albums—and then go hunting around your house for places to tuck them into.

**17** **FILING PLUS** A wide cabinet is ideal for oversize art paper and children's drawings—and it's even more efficient when it features an extra-slim bottom drawer, like the one in this custom-built version.

**18** **PLANNING AHEAD** If you're installing kitchen cabinets, consider this idea for using every square inch of space. Most cabinets are raised 4 or 5 inches off the floor, with a toe kick space beneath. You can fill the space with shallow drawers to hide anything from silver flatware to lightbulbs, or even use it to accommodate a folding stepladder.

**19** **MOVABLE DRAWER** Just a slim drawer on casters, this under-bed bin is an ingenious place to store linens, blankets, or sweaters; keep them protected in zippered bags. While this drawer was constructed of plywood and Douglas fir, you can also find ready-made plastic bins on wheels. Risers are also available to add valuable inches to your under-bed storage space.

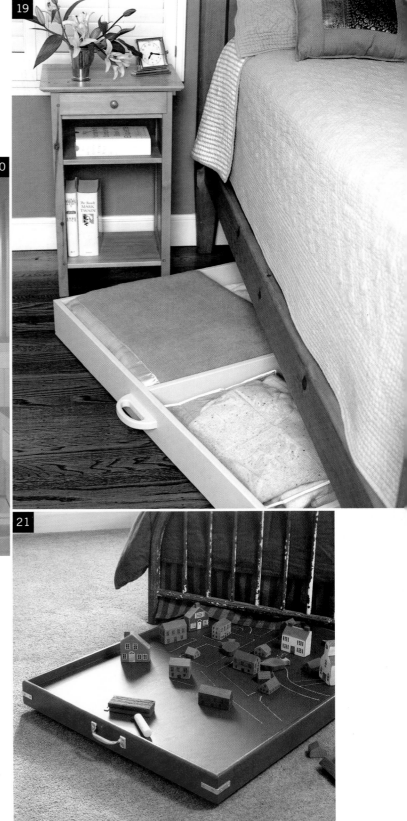

**20** **ALL-IN-ONE STORAGE** Many platform-style beds come with built-in drawers. These are a boon because they keep clothes dust free while making use of that often-overlooked space under the bed. For a more peaceful sleep, however, store financial papers or old tax records elsewhere.

**21** **ROLL-AWAY FUN** This homemade low-profile tray rolls out on casters and rolls right back when it's time for bed. A lip on the edges keeps pieces corralled. The chalkboard-painted surface lets kids draw and redraw a city plan. A larger version could accommodate a model railway.

# hidden assets

Benches and window seats offer a golden opportunity to use the space beneath for storage. Whether the seating you have in mind is freestanding or built-in, plan on including drawers or cubbies, with or without doors. You can achieve a built-in look without all the building by turning several sturdy storage cubes on their sides, screwing them together, painting them, and topping them with an upholstered foam pad. An even easier option is to purchase an ottoman that doubles as a storage unit.

22

**22 DOUBLE DUTY** This handsome built-in window seat is the focal point of a mini-library. It's also a great place to store files. The bench seat lifts up to reveal a divided interior fitted with inserts to hold files. A piano hinge is the secret to the seat's smooth functioning. This arrangement allows for storage without that office look; with the cushion and throw pillows in place, no one's the wiser.

**23**

**23** **OPEN ACCESS** A simple open bench works equally well in an entryway or at the foot of a bed for combined storage and seating. Here, dividers keep contents organized, and a cushioned top adds comfort.

**24** **CUSTOM FILING** Conventional filing cabinets can take up lots of room and may not blend with your home decor. This custom-built bench features pull-out file drawers underneath—they are easy to access, neat and tidy when closed.

**24**

# waste not, store lots

In your search for unused space to claim for storage, don't overlook stairways. Underneath them is a fairly large wedge-shaped area just waiting to be framed in and used for enclosed storage, or left open for shoes, books, coats, or even an office. The walls that flank the stairs can be pressed into service for shallow surface-mounted or recessed shelving.

**25** **OPEN-ENDED** Instead of closing in the wedge beneath the staircase, this solution uses the underside as a unique bookcase. A clever set of ascending niches holds books, artfully arranged and accented with decorative objects in a charming sitting area.

**26** **PRACTICAL PULLOUTS** In a home where closet space was minimal, the owners created two ingenious mini-closets that slide out from under the stairs. One unit has a seat for removing shoes; the other holds coats and boots. The doors' raised paneling matches that of the surrounding room.

**27** **WHOSE SHOES?** The whole family can stash shoes in this roomy under-stairs cubby. Two openings, handsomely framed with door casing to match other trim in the house, accommodate freestanding wooden shoe racks. Handy hooks keep hats ready.

**28** **LIBRARY WALL** Recessed into the wall of a switchback staircase, stepped shelves support books and framed photos. It's an open invitation for readers of all sizes to settle down on the carpeted stairs and page through a favorite book.

27

28

# where anything goes

You can greatly expand your home's storage potential by recognizing and using mostly forgotten spaces—areas around windows and doors, under seating, on the backs of doors, and even up in the rafters. Your main decision will be whether to enclose the found space or use it to display collections.

**29** **BOOK NOOK** When planning a kitchen, create niches out of the areas around doors, above cabinets, and alongside appliances. A narrow column of shelving ekes out just enough room to keep a cookbook collection close at hand, while space over the door displays attractive but useful items.

**30** **LITTLE EXTRAS** Two found spaces—the inside of the pantry closet door and one end of a wall—have been used to provide storage between the kitchen and the dining area. The shelves built onto the pantry door are deep enough for jars and cans. In the foreground, a narrow bookcase holds a surprising number of volumes. Beyond, kitchen cabinets and shelves are tucked under a staircase.

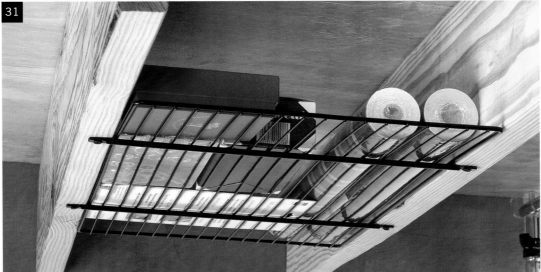

**31** **HEADS UP!** In a workshop, basement, or other utility space, don't overlook what's overhead. Open rafters can be the perfect spots to install wire shelving that can hold rolls of wrapping paper, office supplies, or cleaning products.

**32** **PERSONAL SPACE** In this luxurious bath/dressing room, extra storage space was right in plain sight. A room divider functions as an open closet, with shirts and slacks hung on a rod suspended from the ceiling. Elegant cabinetry below houses folded clothing and accessories.

# high-tech storage

The technological revolution has created a new storage dilemma in the average home—where to put it all? Computers, TVs, DVD players, and speakers all need a place where they won't intrude, and where all those cables and wires can be neatly stashed. Specially designed cabinetry and closet spaces can house the equipment itself, and a new generation of wire-management devices can help with all that electrical "spaghetti."

## 33 SECURITY SYSTEM

Stowed discreetly in a high cabinet at left, this closed-circuit television monitors the driveway approach to the home. The same storage idea could be used to disguise a TV set in a bedroom or den.

33

**34** **MEDIA CLOSET** This closet is the nerve center for the home's entertainment system, keeping it out of sight, dust free, and protected. Wireless enthusiasts can install systems that transmit video and audio signals from cable controllers, satellite receivers, and video recorders to TVs and speakers around the house. Wired or not, be sure the closet has adequate outlets and sufficient ventilation to prevent heat buildup and damage to delicate equipment.

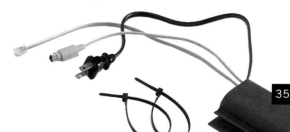

**35** **WRANGLING WIRES**
Among the many devices on the market to keep cables and wires tangle free, two are simple and straightforward. A raceway (right) can mount to a desk, wall, or floor; wires are fed through it and thus neatly stowed. Plastic ties (left) are an inexpensive way to bundle cords; when you want to change the arrangement, just cut the ties and rebundle with new ones.

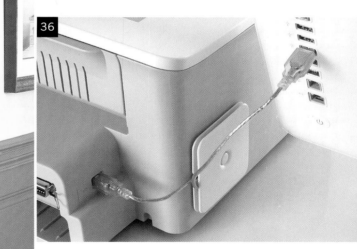

**36** **CORD CONTROL** This nifty device stores up to 6 feet of USB or FireWire cable smartly spiraled inside a streamlined protective case. Mount it on a wall or the side of a monitor or printer, or unclip it to take your laptop on the go.

# don't just store, display!

Why hide away objects you love to look at or use often? Instead, display them proudly and make them an essential element of your room's decor. Storing things in plain sight also means you'll be more likely to remember what you have and put it to use. The key to display storage is twofold: first, create an attractive arrangement by grouping items by use, color, or material; and second, keep everything, including the shelves themselves, clean and dust free. To create a pleasing composition, play with the arrangement, adding and subtracting objects and moving them around until you achieve the effect you're looking for.

**37 THE GEOMETRY OF WINE** When you want to have your favorite vintages ready to pull out for a meal, storing them in the kitchen is the way to go. This custom-built wine cubby makes a pleasing design statement while keeping bottles properly stored on their sides.

**38 COTTAGE STYLE** The combination of red and white is the dominant theme in this country-cottage display of kitchenware. Shaker pegs, painted red and hung vertically, are perfect for displaying matching mugs; enamelware, canisters, and other pieces in daily use complete the charming vignette.

**40** **PICK A CARD** Clear vinyl pockets create a personal stationery store, with greeting cards displayed in slots labeled "Birthday," "New Home," "Engagement," and so on. Simply snap the pockets over a rod, suspend the arrangement from an over-the-door hook, and your "card shop" is open for business.

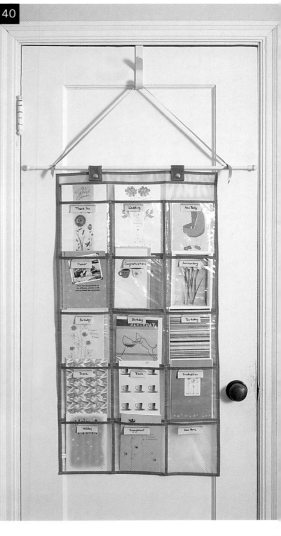

40

**39** **SHIMMER AND SHINE** A vintage metal cabinet is the backdrop for a collection of gleaming silver pieces, beloved bowls, and other decorative objects. What makes the arrangement so appealing is the variation of height and color, combined with the similarities of texture and shape.

# making room for tools

**B**eing organized in the garden is just as important to your peace of mind as keeping order indoors—especially when it comes to all the tools and paraphernalia that gardeners accumulate. From tool racks to sheds, there are plenty of outdoor options available in nurseries, hardware stores, and home-improvement centers to help you get your act together. Besides making it easier to find the tools you need, orderly storage will help keep them dry and in good condition.

**41** **OUTDOOR CLOSETS** In this beautifully planned patio/utility area, bifold doors slide back to reveal a long, shallow recess fitted with all the essentials. A potting sink, counter space, and storage for vases are all close at hand for creating flower arrangements from the cutting garden. Upper shelves are made of boards supported on metal brackets. Potting materials are stored on more shelving in the adjacent closet.

41

**42 UPSTANDING** One of many freestanding tool racks on the market, this tough plastic model provides well-balanced storage for long-handled garden tools and trowels alike. The virtue of a rack like this is that you can stash it in a corner or easily move it elsewhere as tasks demand.

**43 ALL TOGETHER** Built from weather-resistant cedar, this prefab shed features hooks and racks for tools and deep shelves for pots and pruners. There's plenty of floor space for everything from a watering can to a carryall. Double doors open wide for easy access, and a sloped roof allows rain to roll off.

**44 SHOVEL SPACE** This wall-mounted rack is great for compact storage of rakes, shovels, brooms, and other tools.

# resource guide

One of the best things about a closet makeover is that it's a true do-it-yourself project. That said, there are thousands of retailers and professionals who can help you with your makeover. Look for closet systems, hardware, and accessories from home-improvement centers and organizing stores, or go online and search on the words "closet systems" for literally millions of choices.

To help you narrow your search, we've compiled a list of professional organizations, closet consultants, and retailers who we found helpful in the course of putting together this book. We hope you will, too.

## GENERAL REFERENCE

**NATIONAL ASSOCIATION OF PROFESSIONAL ORGANIZERS**
847-375-4746
napo.net

**NATIONAL CLOSET GROUP**
866-624-5463
www.closets.com

## CLOSET SYSTEMS & CONSULTANTS

**CALIFORNIA CLOSETS**
888-336-9709
calclosets.com

**THE CLOSET FACTORY**
800-634-9000
closetfactory.com

**CLOSETMAID**
800-874-0008
closetmaid.com

**CLOSETS TO GO**
888-312-7424
closetstogo.com

**EASYCLOSETS**
800-910-0129
easyclosets.com

**EURODESIGN LTD.**
800-970-7338
eurodesignltd.com

**POLIFORM USA**
888-POLIFORM
poliformusa.com

**SCHULTE DISTINCTIVE STORAGE**
800-669-3225
schultestorage.com

**SHIPSHAPE**
510-533-0375
shipshape.com

**SPRUCE**
510-525-4460
sprucegirls.com

**STUDIO BECKER**
510-865-1616
studiobecker.com

**WINDQUEST COMPANIES, INC.**
800-562-4257
easytrack.com
homeorg.com

## PRODUCTS

**BALLARD DESIGNS**
800-536-7551
ballarddesigns.com

**BED BATH & BEYOND**
800-462-3966
bedbathandbeyond.com

**BLU DOT DESIGN**
612-782-1844
bludot.com

**THE CONTAINER STORE**
800-786-7315
containerstore.com

**DOUGLAS HOMER**
484-883-1804
douglashomer.com

**EXPOSURES**
800-222-4947
exposuresonline.com

**GARNET HILL**
800-870-3513
garnethill.com

**GUIDECRAFT**
800-334-2014
guidecraft.com

**HABLE CONSTRUCTION**
212-228-5942
hableconstruction.com

**HOLD EVERYTHING**
800-421-2264
holdeverything.com

**THE HOME DEPOT**
800-553-3199
homedepot.com

**IKEA**
800-434-4532
ikea-usa.com

**IMPROVEMENTS**
800-642-2112
improvementscatalog.com

**KNAPE & VOGT MANUFACTURING**
800-253-1561
knapeandvogt.com

**LIGHT IMPRESSIONS**
800-828-6216
lightimpressionsdirect.com

**LILLIAN VERNON**
800-901-9402
lillianvernon.com

**LOWE'S**
800-445-6937
lowes.com

**ORGANIZE EVERYTHING**
800-600-9817
organize-everything.com

**ORGANIZE-IT**
800-210-7712
organize-it-online.com

**RUBBERMAID**
888-895-2110
rubbermaid.com

**SMARTHOME**
800-762-7846
smarthome.com

**STACKS AND STACKS**
800-761-5222
stacksandstacks.com

**TARGET**
800-591-3869
target.com

**WINDCHASER**
800-405-2943
windchaserproducts.com

**ACKNOWLEDGMENTS**

Many professionals, businesses, and home-owners assisted us by providing advice and information, or by opening their doors to our photo crew. We would especially like to thank closet owners: Grant K. Gibson Interior Design, Melissa Houtte, Dave Martin, Hannah Mason, Michele Mason, Katherine North of Northbrook Design, and Judith Rosen. Thanks also to *Sunset* magazine; Deborah Silberberg and Sylvia Borchert of ShipShape and ShipShape assistants Larry Aleshire, Christine Hebel, and James Vanoni; Courtney Shaver of The Container Store; Tali Reicher and Rachel Siegel of Spruce; Scott Atkinson; Susan Piper of Piper Design Associates; Linda J. Selden; and stylist assistant Deanna Sison.

**PHOTOGRAPHERS**

**Jean Allsopp:** 33 all, 61 top right; **Ron Anderson/ Gloria Gale:** 106 left, 114 right; **Scott Atkinson:** 11 bottom right, 83 bottom, 92 bottom right; **Brian Vanden Brink:** 32 top, 54–55 center, 55 right, 62, 64 top right, 89, 100, 111 left, 118, 122; **Caesar-Stone:** 80 top; **James Carrier:** 51 bottom right, 75 right, 109 left; **Todd Caverly:** 20 bottom, 40 left, 90 bottom left; **ClosetMaid Corp.:** 12; **Crandall & Crandall:** 110 bottom; **Phillip Ennis:** 119 left; **Cheryl Fenton:** 32 bottom; **Frank Gaglione:** 21 all, 43 right, 111 top right; **Tria Giovan:** 27 top, 28 all, 30 bottom, 35 top left, 64 bottom, 91 top, 95 left, 99 middle right, 107 bottom; **Laurey W. Glenn:** 24 all, 47 top left, 60 all, 94 top; **Jay Graham:** 104 bottom, 110 top; **John Granen:** 108 right; **Jamie Hadley:** 63 bottom right, 82 top right, 85, 120 left; **Margot Hartford:** 2–3 center bottom, 61 bottom left, 102, 105 left, 115 top, 116 right, 121 left; **Philip Harvey:** 34, 63 center right, 119 top right; **Alex Hayden:** 54 bottom left, 93 top, 115 bottom; **Muffy Kibbey:** 36 and 37, 61 bottom right; daviddduncanlivingston.com: 2 center, 50, 106 right; **Kathryn MacDonald:** 73 bottom left; **Bill Mathews/Gloria Gale:** 46 top right, 68, 82 top left and bottom; **E. Andrew McKinney:** 41 top and bottom, 42 bottom left, 91 bottom, 111 bottom right; **Susan Gentry McWhinney:** 113 right; **John O'Hagan:** 29 all, 43 left, 47 top right, 95 top right, 107 top; **Bradley Olman:** 42 top, 46 bottom; **David Papazian:** 51 bottom left; **David Prince:** 2 bottom center, 76 all; **Eric Roth:** 20 top, 103, 109 bottom, 117 bottom; **Mark Rutherford:** 80 bottom, 83 top left, 83 top right, 86, 88, 90 right top to bottom, 93 bottom; **David Schiff,** 11 bottom left; **Michael Shopenn:** 114 left; **Dan Stultz:** 11 center; **Thomas J. Story:** 69 top right, 72 bottom, 75 top left, 94 bottom, 104 top; **Tim Street-Porter:** 109 top right; **Luca Trovato:** 3 center, 57 center left, 65; **David Wakely:** 72 top right, 112 top right; **Jessie Walker:** 73 top right, 112 left, bottom right; **Michele Lee Willson:** 2 center left and bottom left, 2–3 center top and center, 3 top center, 5 all, 6, 7, 8, 13 top left, 14–15 all, 16–17 all, 18–19 all, 22 bottom right, 23, 38–39 all, 44–45 all, 48–49 all, 56, 57 bottom left and bottom right, 58–59 all, 66–67 all, 69 bottom left, 70–71 all, 81, 95 bottom right, 121 all, 124, 125, 128; **Sylvia Martin Windam:** 77 left, 116 left; **Ben Woolsey:** 105 bottom right

**ILLUSTRATORS**

If not otherwise credited, illustrations are by **Tracy La Rue Hohn**
**Melanie Magee:** 74; **Bill Oetinger:** 80

## ARCHITECTS & DESIGNERS

2 (center left) Styling: Julie Maldonado 2 (center) Design: Mercedes Corbell Design & Architecture (mercedescorbelldesign.com) 2 (bottom left) Design: ShipShape; Styling: Laura Del Fava 2–3 (top center) Styling: Laura Del Fava 2–3 (center) Styling: Laura Del Fava; Glass jars: Target; Woven boxes: Cost Plus 2–3 (bottom center) Architect: Fox Design Group, Architects (foxdesigngroup.com); Interior Design: Navarra Design Inc. (navarradesign.com) 3 (top right) Styling: Laura Del Fava 4 Design: California Closets 5 (top right) Design: ShipShape; Styling: Laura Del Fava; Paint: Benjamin Moore #2017-20; Bins, Casserole dividers: IKEA 5 (bottom left) Styling: Laura Del Fava 5 (bottom right) Styling: Julie

Maldonado 13 (top left) Design: ShipShape; Styling: Laura Del Fava; Bins: The Container Store; Box: Target; Document boxes: IKEA 13 (top right) Design: California Closets 14 (left center and bottom left) Design: ShipShape 15 Design: ShipShape; Styling: Laura Del Fava; Wire shelving, Wire drawer tower, Wrapping paper organizer, Collapsible bins, Clear photo boxes: The Container Store; Bin (top shelf): Target 16 Design: ShipShape; Styling: Laura Del Fava; Bins: The Container Store; Box: Target 17 Styling: Laura Del Fava 18 (bottom right) Design: ShipShape; Styling: Laura Del Fava; Shoe rack: Crate and Barrel; Tray: Target; Clear boxes: Organized Living 19 (top) Design: ShipShape; Styling: Laura Del Fava 22 (bottom) and 23 Styling: Laura Del Fava 26 Design: California

Closets 27 (center right) Jewelry drawer: Studio Becker 27 (bottom right) Sock organizer: Lillian Vernon 27 (bottom left) Scarf hanger: Organize Everything 30 (top) Shoe rack: Organize Everything 31 (top left) Hanging canvas shelves: Organize-It 31 (top right) Wood shoe cubby: Organize Everything 31 (bottom center) Over-door shoe rack: Organize Everything 31 (bottom right) Flowered shoe holder: Garnet Hill 32 (bottom) Design: Larry Fox of Valet Organizers 34 Design: Remick Associates Architects-Builders, Inc.; Glass artist: Masaoka Glass Design (alanmasaoka.com) 35 (top right) Slacks hangers: The Container Store 35 (middle right) Tie caddy: Organize Everything 35 (lower right) Tie drawer: Studio Becker 35 (bottom right) Design: California Closets 36–37 Cabinet Design: John T. Hewitt Jr./Cabinet Crafters 38 (left) and 39 (top) Shelves and bins: The Container Store 40–41 (center) Design: California Closets 41 (top) Design: Heidi M. Emmett 41 (bottom) Design: Norm Claybaugh/Creative Interiors 42 (bottom) Design: Melissa Beyeler with design consultant Heather Stone for Imagine That 44 (bottom) and 45 (all) Styling: Julie Maldonado; Bins, Photo drawers: The Container Store; Shelves: The Home Depot 47 (bottom left) Wheeled cart: The Container Store 48 (right) and 49 (top) Design: ShipShape; Styling: Laura Del Fava; Bins: The Container Store; Boxes, Magazine holders: IKEA 50 Design: Mercedes Corbell Design & Architecture (mercedes corbelldesign.com) 52 Photo boxes, albums: Exposures 53 (top left) Media carousel: Guidecraft 53 (bottom right) Crates: Ballard Designs 54 (left) Design: Dan Nelson/Design Northwest Architects 56 Design: ShipShape; Styling: Laura Del Fava; Wire shelving, Wrapping paper organizer, Collapsible bins, Clear photo boxes: The Container Store; Bin (top shelf) : Target 57 (bottom left) Styling: Laura Del Fava 57 (bottom right) Styling: Julie Maldonado; Bins, Photo drawers: The Container Store; Shelves: The Home Depot 58 (bottom) and 59 (all) Design: ShipShape; Styling: Laura Del Fava; Glass jars: Target; Bamboo wine caddy, Woven boxes: Cost Plus 60 Styling: Lisa Powell 61 (top right) Design: Harrell Remodeling, Design & Build (harrell-remodeling.com) 61 (bottom right) Design: C. David Robinson Architects 63 (center left and bottom left) Studio Becker 63 (center right) Interior Design: Studio Becker/ Steven W. Sanborn 63 (bottom right) Design: Eurodesign Ltd. 66–67 (all) Design: Grant K. Gibson Interior Design (grantkgibson.com) 69 (bottom) Design: Grant K. Gibson Interior Design (grantkgibson.com) 70 (bottom) and 71 (all) Design: ShipShape; Styling: Laura Del Fava; Paint: Benjamin Moore #2017-20; Bins, Casserole dividers: IKEA 72 (bottom) Architect: Dale Gardon Design LLC; Interior design: Tamm

Jasper Interiors **72** (top) Design: Jim O'Neill/OZ Architects **73** (bottom) Design: Malcolm Davis **79** Container: Hable Construction **81** (top) Design: ShipShape; Styling: Laura Del Fava; **87** Wardrobe: IKEA **92** (top left and right) Lights: Improvements **92** (bottom left) Automatic light: Smarthome **93** (top) Design: Dan Nelson/ Design Northwest Architects **94** (left) Design: Lindy Small Architecture **95** (bottom right) Design: ShipShape; Styling: Laura Del Fava **96** (left) Stackable cubes: Douglas Homer **96** (top right) Cabinet: Blu Dot **96** (bottom right) Bins: IKEA **97** (top left) Baskets: Lillian Vernon **97** (top right) Zippered bin: Oriac **97** (bottom right and left) Canvas containers: Hable Construction **98** Closet system: IKEA **99** (top) Organizing pieces: Bed Bath and Beyond **99** (middle left) Oriac **99** (bottom) Jewelry organizer: Organize-It **101** (top right) Air purifier: Improvements **101** (top left) Cedar products: Improvements **101** (bottom left) Air purifier: Windchaser **101** (bottom right) Sachets: Gump's **102** Architect: David S. Gast & Associates, Architects (dsga.com); Design: Carol White **103** Design: Astrid Vigeland **105** (top right) Overdoor rack: Lillian Vernon **105** (left) Architect: Fox Design Group, Architects (foxdesigngroup.com); Interior Design: Navarra Design Inc. (navarradesign. com) **108** (bottom left) Étagère: Lillian Vernon **108** (bottom right) Design: SkB Architects (skbarchitects.com) **110** (top) Design: Michele Dutra/Custom Kitchens by John Wilkins **111** (bottom right) Design: Debra S. Weiss **111** (left) Design: Donham & Sweeny Architects **112** (top) Design: Kevin Patrick O'Brien & Janice Stone Thomas **113** (bottom right) Design: Kevin Patrick O'Brien & Janice Stone Thomas **114** (left) Design: Charles Wooldridge **115** (top) Design: Ronald W. Madson/Madson Associates **115** (bottom) Design: David Pelletier/Pelletier + Schaar for Designs Northwest **116** (top) Architect: David S. Gast & Associates, Architects (dsga.com); Design: Carol White **117** (top) Rack: Sporty's **119** (bottom right) Cable holder: Organize Everything **120** (top) Architect: Fox Design Group, Architects (foxdesigngroup.com) **120** (bottom) Design: Christine Worboys **121** (left) Styling: Laura Del Fava **121** (right) Styling: Julie Maldonado **123** (top right) Tool stand: Rubbermaid **123** (bottom right) Tool rack: The Container Store **123** (left) Garden hutch: Smith & Hawken **124** Design: ShipShape; Styling: Laura Del Fava **125** Shelves and bins: The Container Store **128** Design: ShipShape; Styling: Laura Del Fava; Bins: The Container Store; Boxes: IKEA

## RETAILERS & MANUFACTURERS

We would like to thank the following for giving us permission to feature their photography: Ballard Designs: **53** bottom right; Bed, Bath and Beyond: **99** top right; Blu Dot: **96** top right; California Closets: **4, 13** top right, **26, 35** bottom right; **40–41** center; ClosetMaid Corporation: **12, 78, 84** all; The Container Store: **35** top right, **47** bottom left, **123** bottom right; Douglas Homer: **96** left; Eurodesign Ltd.: **63** bottom right; Exposures: **52** top; Garnet Hill: **31** bottom right; Guidecraft: **43** top right; Hable Construction: **79, 97** bottom right, **97** bottom left; IKEA: **87, 96** bottom right, **99;** Improvements: **92** top left, **101** top left, top right; Lillian Vernon: **27** bottom right, **97** top left, **105** top right, **108** bottom left; Organize Everything: **27** bottom left, **31** top right and center bottom; **35** middle right, **119** bottom right; Organize-It: **31** top left, **99** bottom left; Oriac: **97** top right, **99** middle left; Rubbermaid: **123** top right; Schulte Distinctive Storage: **Cover;** Smarthome: **92** bottom left; Smith & Hawken: **123** bottom left; Sporty's: **117** top; Studio Becker: **27** center right; **35** lower right, **63** center left, bottom left, and center right, **63** bottom right; Windchaser: **101** bottom left

# index